Mind Maps®
for
Business

Mind Maps® for
Business

Revolutionise your business thinking and practice

Tony Buzan™

with Chris Griffiths

and James Harrison, consultant editor

Harlow, England • London • New York • Boston • San Francisco • Toronto • Sydney • Singapore • Hong Kong
Tokyo • Seoul • Taipei • New Delhi • Cape Town • Madrid • Mexico City • Amsterdam • Munich • Paris • Milan

Published by BBC Active, an imprint of Educational Publishers LLP, part of the Pearson Education Group, Edinburgh Gate, Harlow, Essex CM20 2JE, England.

First published in Great Britain in 2010

ISBN: 978-1-4066-4290-2

British Library Cataloguing-in-Publication Data
A catalogue record for this book is available from the British Library

Library of Congress Cataloging-in-Publication Data
Buzan, Tony.
  Mind maps for business : revolutionise your business thinking and practice / Tony Buzan ; with Chris Griffiths and James Harrison, consultant editor. -- 1st ed.
    p. cm.
  Includes index.
  ISBN 978-1-4066-4290-2 (pbk.)
  1. Success in business. 2. Intellect. 3. Brain. 4. Thought and thinking. I. Griffiths, Chris. II. Harrison, James. III. Title.
  HF5386.B9545 2009
  658.4001'9--dc22
                          2009038566

10 9 8 7 6 5 4 3 2 1
13 12 11 10 09

Text design by Design Deluxe
Typeset in 9.5 Swis721 Lt BT by 30
Printed and bound by Ashford Colour Press Ltd, Gosport, Hants

The publisher's policy is to use paper manufactured from sustainable forests.

To Nicky, Strilli and Jonathan Oppenheimer,
who were so significant in helping to make
the Mind Map dream come true.

Contents

Part 4 Mind Mapping for better business outcomes 209

Foreword

I came to mind mapping late in life – despite knowing Tony for many years and the fact that my wife had been an early convert. My problem was one of aesthetics. The Mind Maps that I attempted looked so bad in comparison to those of Tony's and my wife's, both in fluidity of lines and clarity of pictures, that I let my embarrassment cloud my better judgement. However, recently, software has become available which can draw those lines and pictures for you and I now realise how shortsighted and feeble I had been in not embracing Mind Maps for business sooner. Since my conversion I have found Mind Maps to be an indispensable aid to me in the business world and I would recommend this book and what it proposes to all businesspeople.

Nicky Oppenheimer, Chairman, De Beers

Note: To see a Mind Map used as a business application by De Beers, see page 139.

Acknowledgements

Authors' acknowledgements

This has been a truly global enterprise with Mind Map business examples, stories and contributions pouring in from all corners of the planet. Across the globe, I pass on my sincerest *thank yous* to:

Nicky Oppenheimer for his foreword and his De Beers Organisation Mind Map; to HSH Prince Philipp of Liechtenstein for his friendship and support of Mind Maps through his LGT-Academy, and for providing the story thereof; to Masanori Kanda, Mikiko Chikada Kawase, Ken Ito, Shiro Kobayashi and Masato Uchiyama Sensei, for their utter dedication to and support of the Mind Maps in Business project and for the fascinating Japanese Mind Map stories they translated and provided; to Seijo Naito and to the Sports Managers College operated by the Japan Football Association for their much appreciated Mind Map input; to His Excellency Dr Abdul Hussein Ali Mirza, Minister for Oil and Gas, Bahrain, for his stirring endorsement, and to Sheikh Hamad bin Ebrahim Al Khalifa for his total support of the Mind Map idea and for his profound insight of it, as exemplified by his Intelnacom Mind Map; to Jorge O. Castañeda, President of Buzan Latin America, for his pioneering work and for his editorial support; to Hilde Jaspaert at Buzan Europe for mind-mapping expertise and ongoing support; to Ram Ganglani and Gautam Ganglani (Chairman and Managing Director respectively) of Right Selection LLC Group in Dubai for their excellent iMindMaps; to Henry Toi and Eric Cheong at Buzan Asia for their incredible ongoing support right from the start of the project and to Thum Cheng Cheong and Lim Choon Boo in Singapore, Kwon Bong Jung and Park Sang Hoon in South Korea, Tanya Phonanan in Thailand, and Po Chung in Hong Kong also for their invaluable Mind Map contributions; to Bill Jarrard and Jennifer Goddard at Buzan Centre Australia/New Zealand for their superb input and for being such shining examples of the success of Mind Maps in Business; to Jaime Baird for his New Zealand Mind Maps; to Al Homyk, Dave Hill and Lisa Frigand at Con Edison for the amazing 9/11 Mind Map story; to Dr Mike Stanley for the Boeing Mind Map success story; to John J. Ryall MD, Ryall Development Training Ltd, Ireland, for his inspiring Mind Map story.

My thanks also to Bruce Johnstone of Fidelity Investments for exemplifying the use of Mind Map in finance; to Dr Stephen Lundin for his creative journey as a Mind Mapper, and *FISH!* and *CAT* best-selling author; to Anthony J. Mento, and Raymond M. Jones, of Loyola College, and Patrick Matinelli of Johns Hopkins University, on their executive MBA programme and insights into Mind Mapping; and to Kathleen Kelly, Management Professor and consultant.

A special 'virtual' thank you to Chuck Frey the pre-eminent Mind Map blogger who created the Mind Map 'Communications Centres' at **http://mindmapping. typepad.com** and **http://mindmappingsoftwareblog.com** and for permission to quote from his blogs.

Back in the UK I must thank firstly and foremostly my co-author and friend Chris Griffiths, Chief Executive of Buzan Online Ltd, whose extraordinary genius, commitment, persistence and belief in Mind Maps and Mental Literacy gave birth to first, the prodigiously intelligent iMindMap software, and second, to much of the inspiration for this book. Fantastic visual and text support was also provided by Emily Van Keogh and Melina Costi at Buzan Online and the team based in Cardiff, including Owen Hardy.

Thank you also to Raymond Keene OBE, and Chess Grandmaster and Mind Sports Correspondent for *The Times* for his indefatigable steer and support; and to Brian Lee for being a friend and stalwart in helping me to bring Mind Maps to the business world; to Phil Chambers who created many of the Mind Maps and is the reigning Mind Mapping World Champion; he has been a Senior Buzan Licensed Instructor since 1995 and runs Mind Mapping and other seminars and courses. He can be contacted at **www.learning-tech.co.uk**

My thanks to James Harrison, our diligent and consultant editor, who brought so much of this book to life.

Without my 'home team' at Buzan H.Q. this book would have been a logistical nightmare: therefore a heartfelt thank you must go to Pauline Aleski, Anne Reynolds, Suzi Rockett and Jenny Redman for fantastic logistical support and effort. Thank you also to Tim Fulford for his runner illustrations.

At Pearson, the publishers, I would like to thank Richard Stagg, Director, who was a prime figure in the launching of this project; and to add my profound thanks to Samantha Jackson, my cherished Commissioning Editor, for her total commitment to Mind Maps and to this book throughout its long gestation; also to her team in Harlow – Caroline Jordan, Barbara Massam and Emma Devlin.

Last, and certainly not least, my acknowledgements to all those mind-mapping businesspeople and educators who enthusiastically provided Mind Maps and stories, both for the first edition and this revised and updated edition, and whom for reasons of space I have either omitted to thank or been unable to include.

Thank you also to Michael Porter Organisation for permission to use their five forces framework and value chain processes, to Boston Consulting Group for their growth-share matrix and to McKinsey & Co for their 7-S framework.

Lastly, dear reader, a special thanks to you for joining the growing global community of Mind Map practitioners in business. PLEASE do contact me with your business and work-related Mind Maps and stories for possible inclusion in the next edition of *Mind Maps for Business* at **tony.buzan@buzanworld.com**.

Tony Buzan

A book of this nature is the product of the efforts of many people. First, I would like to thank my co-author Tony Buzan, who has, through exceptional vision, wisdom and friendship, shaped my life for the better. It is rare to meet an individual who can make a profound difference to the way you live your life. Tony is one of those people.

I am especially grateful to two of my longstanding colleagues, Emily and Melina, for their dedication and hard work: this book could not have been completed without them. To James, the supreme juggler, for taking on the seemingly impossible task of pulling everything together. To Brian, for steering the ship so well. To Phil, for his great artistic skills. To the entire genius team at Buzan Online, to whom I would like to say an especially big thank you for working so tirelessly to make the iMindMap dream a reality for so many. To my family for making me who I am. Most of all, to my wife Gaile, and my wonderfully amazing children Alex and Abbie, for their love and support. Nothing is more important to me. And finally to Ron, my friend and sounding board, whose late-night conversations over many a glass of red wine will be sadly missed.

Chris Griffiths

Publisher's acknowledgements

The publisher would like to thank the following for permission to reproduce copyright material. While every effort has been made to trace and acknowledge all copyright holders, we would like to apologise should there have been any errors or omissions.

Mind Maps

The Mind Maps remain the copyright of their owners as listed below.

Phil Chambers for the contents overview Mind Map and the mini chapter opener Mind Maps throughout the book; Ram Ganglani and Gautam Ganglani page xxi; Prince Philipp of Liechtenstein pages 11 and 12; Park Sang Hoon page 74; Seijo Naito page 93; Jaimie Baird pages 103 and 123; Lim Choon Boo page 110; Dr M. Stanley/Boeing page 115; Henry Toi page 119; Hilde Jaspaert page 121, Master Buzan™ Trainer for Mind Mapping and Speed Reading, hilde@inter-activeminds.com; Al Homyk, Dave Hill and Lisa Frigand at Con Edison pages 130, 131 and 132 © Con Edison; De Beers page 139; Jennifer Goddard page 140; Jim Messerschmitt and Tony Messina at EDS pages 143 and 144; Masanori Kanda pages 151 and 153; Stephen Lundin page 161; Digital Equipment Corp page 167; Sheikh Hamad page

203; Thum Cheng Cheong page 232; The Japan Football Association page 239, with kind permission; Mikiko Chikada Kawase page 240.

Photographs

Henry Toi and Buzan Asia pages 117 and 118; Masanori Kanda page 151; Tome City Office pages 169 and 170, with kind permission; The Japan Football Association page 238, with kind permission.

Figures

Adam Hart-Davis / Science Photo Library for the figure on page 10; POD/ Photodisc. StockTrek for the figure on page 17; Chuck Frey for use of the chart on page 40. Chuck is the author of **www.mindmappingsoftwareblog.com**; Harvard Business Review and the Michael Porter Organisation for Porter's Five Forces model on page 182 and the Balanced Scorecard on page 187; The Boston Consulting Group for the BCG Portfolio Matrix on page 190; Simon & Schuster for Porter's Value Chain figure on page 192; McKinsey & Company for the McKinsey 7-S framework on page 195.

The authors would also like to offer their special thanks to Dr Stanley and Boeing for allowing the reproduction of Dr Stanley in front of his Mind Map masterpiece! (See page 115.)

Preface

*Most of us now live in an 'information democracy' ... But while
we've gone a long way towards optimizing how we use information,
we haven't yet done the same for knowledge ... 'Mind Mapping'
software can also be used as a digital 'blank slate' to help connect
and synthesize ideas and data – and ultimately create new
knowledge ... and mental models to help people mine and assess
the value of all that information.*

BILL GATES, 'The Road Ahead: How "intelligent agents" and Mind Mappers are
taking our information democracy to the next stage', Newsweek, 25 January 2006

When the world's best-known entrepreneur, founder of the world's richest
philanthropic institution and co-creator of the personal computer revolution
starts talking about Mind Maps and the Knowledge Revolution, you have to
sit up and take notice.

Bill Gates is a man with considerable brainpower, as well as being the co-
founder, chairman and chief software architect of Microsoft Corporation, the
world's largest computer software company. His clarion call is highly pre-
scient. President Vicente Fox of Mexico, in his address to the fifth annual
United Nations Conference on Quality and Innovation, declared that the
twenty-first century was to be the century for the development of intellectual
capital and innovation and should be entitled the Century of the Brain. His
foresight was exemplary; his vision correct.

The rise and rise of intellectual capital

As the global economic downturn continues, the urgent need for better
thinking, memory and creativity is coming to the fore for businesses and
organisations. We are witnessing the downturn of political capital, financial
capital, stocks and shares capital, oil capital and property capital. But
throughout these precipitous and dangerous declines runs the accelerating,
indeed exponential, rise of another form of capital which is hardly reported
at all in the international and global business media: intellectual capital. The
currency of this intellectual capital is intelligence.

The pundits have stated that the economic crisis will see a shift from the
West to the East in terms of business and transfers of capital. This is to see

the situation in a very limited way; the credit crisis is actually global and what it has really highlighted is the beginning of the inevitable and ongoing transition from the Industrial and Information Ages to the Age of Intelligence.

Entering the Age of Intelligence

Since the dawn of civilisation, the world has gone through a number of 'revolutions of the mind', each one shorter than the one preceding it, and each one accelerating exponentially massive changes in the way we work, do business, think and live.

After the Agricultural Revolution came the dynamic Industrial Revolution, which whizzed by in a mere 200 years and heralded an Industrial Age that, with its emphasis on the machine, transformed the business and commercial world. This revolution gave rise to machines that could replicate thought: the telephone, printing press, radio, film, television and the computer. Suddenly the world was awash with data, and the Industrial Revolution created its own Information Revolution. But contrary to what many believe, the Information Age was not the last stage in human evolution but the exposure of a massive seam of information. This led to the frightening reality of 'information overload' and the consequent realisation that something more was needed than simply infinite volumes of data. The short-lived Information Age, less than 100 years from its birth to its transformation, gave birth to a new way of thinking – the Age of Intelligence.

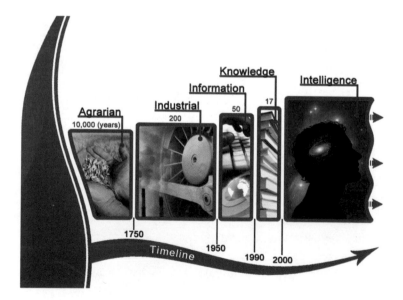

From 2006 to 2009, as part of our lecture circuit on mind mapping, we have been conducting field surveys around the world asking respondents which 'Age' they think we are in now. With virtually no exceptions, the response has been the 'Information Age' or 'Technological Age', or both. That is what people think they are living in, and if they think they are in an 'Age' that they are not in, they are like a fish on land – responses are misdirected and inappropriate.

A few forward thinkers (including Bill Gates) have realised that we are no longer in the Information Age, because information itself was not the 'cure-all' or 'solution' but rather gave rise to its own massive tsunami of information overload that caused confusion and stress. The Age we are now in, born of the Information Age, is the Age of Intelligence.

In order to improve our way of working and conducting business, and in order to make it more effective, we have to change infinite 'bites' of information into something meaningful. In other words, we need to use our intelligence to process the information. To do this we need to know how to use our brain effectively – to use our memory, to think creatively – and this is where Mind Maps come in.

Go create with Mind Maps

Working creatively is essential in any line of business, and using imagination and association helps to produce multiple ideas which can then be fully assessed and analysed. The very best of these innovations can be processed and turned into new strategies, products or services. The Mind Map is an invaluable and innovative way of maximising this creative process; its visually graphic approach triggers your imagination and association, thus powerfully boosting your creativity and memory and leading the Mind Mapper to explore ideas and solutions to problems that previously they might not have considered.

Whatever your burning issue – whether to solve a business problem, find new ways of working, marketing, creating sales, restructuring your business – we firmly believe that the Mind Map is the answer to the many questions you are asking *now*. We fundamentally believe that using Mind Maps is simply a better, more effective approach to maximising your business potential. Your investment in intellectual capital and the Mind Map is one that is well worth making; it will open up infinite professional and personal opportunities and lead you to success!

Tony Buzan and Chris Griffiths, 2009

Introduction

Tony Buzan is a man on an impressive mission – to unlock the power of our brains and show mankind how to tap and use his creative genius with ease and effectiveness. For more than three decades, Tony Buzan has been tireless in his quest to bring this powerful tool to the world. By the latest estimates, about 200 million people around the world are now using Mind Maps, so it is just a matter of time before Mind Maps become a universally used technique.

HIS EXCELLENCY DR ABDUL HUSSEIN ALI MIRZA, Minister for Oil and Gas, Bahrain

Mind mapping is a powerful skill that, once learned, will revolutionise your business practice and the way in which you work. Why is it so powerful? Because creating a Mind Map requires 'whole-brain' synergetic thinking, a process that reflects the explosive nature of the neurons zapping across your brain in search of new connections during the process of thinking. Put more simply, a Mind Map allows your brain to function like some vast pinball machine with billions of silver balls whizzing at the speed of light from flipper to flipper.

Your brain does not think linearly or sequentially like a computer; it thinks multilaterally, 'radiantly'. When you create a Mind Map the branches grow outwards from the central image to form another level of sub-branches, encouraging you to create more ideas out of each thought you add – just as your brain does. And because all the ideas on Mind Maps are linked to each other, your brain is able to make great leaps of understanding and imagination through association.

Mind Maps are the ultimate thinking tool to unlock your brainpower; they reflect the internal Mind Maps of your brain. If you have lost sight of your organisational goals, or your bigger business picture has become blurred, drawing a Mind Map will provide an overview of the situation that will bring clarity and potential to the forefront.

How can Mind Maps help your business?

Mind Maps can revolutionise the way you run your business on a day-to-day basis, allowing you to really think about a situation from every angle in a way that is concise and, importantly, does not waste precious time.

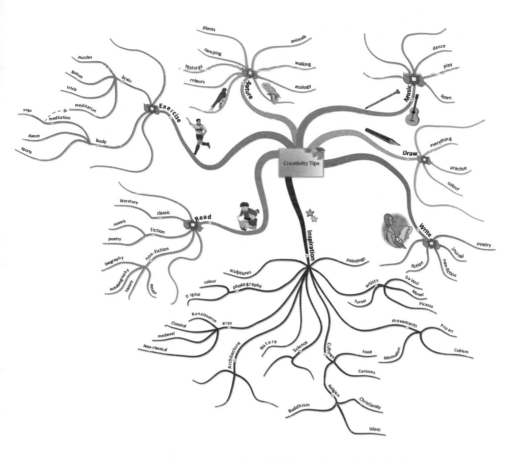

A computer-based Mind Map (created using iMindMap software) showing how cre-ativity can be harnessed and developed. Business thrives on creativity; it is a vital skill that generates new approaches

Mind Maps can be used by every individual in a business or professional organisation in any situation where linear notes would normally be taken. For example, in the morning you can plan your day, week or month using a Mind Map diary. As the day goes on, you can mind map your telephone calls, meetings, brainstorming sessions, team planning events, presentations and interviews. (Subsequent chapters will go into more detail about how to use Mind Maps in specific situations that might arise during your business day.)

In general, Mind Maps facilitate the core business skills – such as making choices; organising your own and other people's ideas; individual and group creativity; analysis; defining and solving problems; setting time and amount targets; and especially memory and communication – all the elements that are essential for successful business management.

By using Mind Maps in their training courses, companies like Boeing, British Petroleum, Digital Computers and EDS have already found that they can make huge savings – in some cases cutting as much as 80 per cent of their overall expenditure. In addition to increasing the speed and efficiency of learning, Mind Maps overcome the usual memory-loss curve, whereby 80 per cent of the detail you have learnt is forgotten within 24 hours. Reviewing Mind Maps at regular intervals ensures that everything learned is both retained and utilised by your brain.

Mind mapping doesn't have to cost you money, either. All you need is paper and pens and you can be on the first step to thinking more success-fully in business.

The Right Selection LLC Group, Dubai

The Right Selection LLC Group, Dubai, UAE, was launched in 1993 with a passion to introduce Training and Development Initiatives to companies in the Gulf region, with a commitment to promote a learning culture within their organisations.

By using Mind Maps we saved each of our executives at least four to five hours a week – a huge amount of time for any organisation.

They helped us to complete projects on time, while avoiding the usual last-minute stress.

Mind Maps made it easier for us to identify resources, delegate, manage and priori-tise tasks effectively, and they helped us to make better choices and set realistic deadlines.

Mind Maps enabled us to capture key points in presentations and organise the flow of the message. Instead of days, presentations took hours or minutes to develop – as everything is on one page the presentation is easy to access, resulting in a clear and powerful message.

Our company's clarity on objectives, knowledge management, customer care ini-tiatives and sales and marketing strategies has been founded on the constant use of Mind Maps.

Mind Mapping is a simple technique with far-reaching benefits the more we implement it.

RAM GANGLANI, Chairman, Right Selection LLC Group
GAUTAM GANGLANI, Managing Director, Right Selection LLC Group
www.rightselection.com/default.aspx

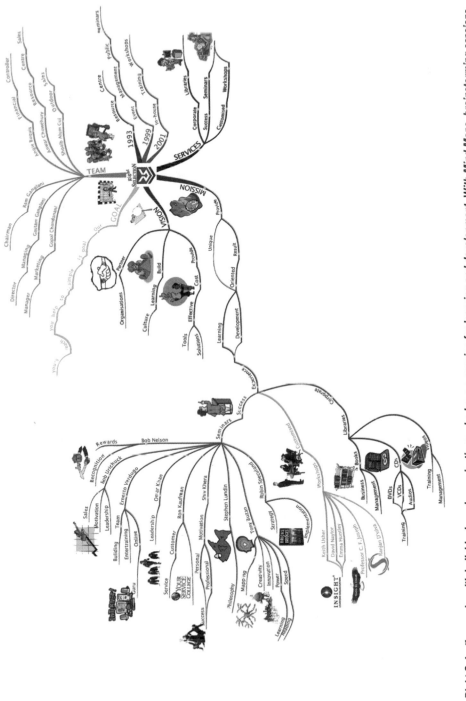

Right Selection works with individuals and organisations who have a passion for learning and development. With Mind Maps, brainstorming sessions are more fun and engaging

How to use this book – a quick Mind Map through the chapters

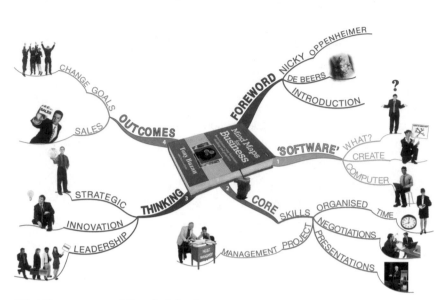

Mind Map summary of the whole book

Part 1: Chapters 1–3

The first three chapters of this book will introduce you to the concept of the Mind Map, set out to explain the thinking behind this powerful and liberating tool, and show you how you can create a Mind Map correctly and share it with business colleagues or clients. Throughout these chapters we will give plenty of step-by-step guides and other examples to help illustrate how the technique can help you and your business, featuring both hand-created and computer-generated Mind Maps.

Part 2: Chapters 4–7

Once you've got to grips with the concept of Mind Maps, Part 2 will explore how you can use Mind Maps within core business skills to streamline your company and strategies; from macro information management and micro note-taking, to planning your time and managing your diary. This section also shows how Mind Maps can facilitate communication and negotiation between individuals, in the boardroom and across companies, and explains how Mind Maps can help you avoid misunderstandings and settle disputes.

Chapter 6 will demonstrate how you can successfully use Mind Maps to deliver presentations and, with the latest computer program, integrate Mind Maps with standard presentation and project management software.

Part 3: Chapters 8–10

Moving on from individual usage, these chapters will show you how you can get the whole company Mind Mapping; encouraging colleagues and staff to use Mind Maps to unite team members in a shared vision, to motivate individuals, or simply for effective delegation of tasks. As Mind Maps are critical for sparking better business thinking (which, as previously stressed, is vital in the Age of Intelligence where intellectual capital is the prime commodity), these chapters demonstrate how you can use them for ideas generation, brainstorming and creative solutions.

Part 4: Chapters 11–12

These chapters show you how to mind map for better business outcomes through sales and through growth and profitability. As a much-needed de-stresser for the end of the day, the final pages of this book provide information on how to mind map the balance between personal and business goal-setting, and how to manage change using Mind Maps.

Throughout the book you will find templates for many Mind Map applications in business, but this is not just a how-to manual for business; it aims to lead by example, showing how Mind Maps have been applied in a host of case studies around the globe – from Bahrain to the blogosphere, from civic leaders to CEOs (ex-Vice President Al Gore uses them for coordinating his climate protection, sustainable investment and other business activities). Stories of the application of Mind Maps take us from strategy planning by the Japanese Soccer Association to coordinating the rebuilding of downtown Manhattan after 9/11, to briefing New Zealand's International Defence Force on biosecurity issues.

Mind Maps have come of age in relation to strategic thinking; they provide an alternative that is easier to follow than standard business processes, such as scenario planning, SWOT, and other popular business models. This book will illustrate how Mind Maps have been harnessed by business professionals and leaders all over the world to improve the productivity and performance of their companies or organisations. Most importantly, read on and you'll find out exactly how you too can use one of the most powerful tools in business today. Welcome to *Mind Maps for Business* and a new way of managing your business thinking and practice.

Online support

 Mind Maps For Business is supported by the **www.MindMapsFor Business.com** website and the iMindMap mind-mapping software.

The online Mind Maps For Business Resource Centre is packed full of useful, informative and interesting mind-mapping materials all for FREE! Access our diverse mind-mapping library TODAY and make sure you download your FREE Mind Mapping Software Trial.

Mind Mapping is a **creativity- and productivity- enhancing** technique that can improve the **learning and efficiency** of individuals and organisations. It is a revolutionary system for **capturing ideas and insights** horizontally on paper.

Anthony J. Mento and Raymond M. Jones, Loyola College, and Patrick Matinelli, Johns Hopkins University, on their executive MBA programme

Part 1
Mind Maps: the ultimate business 'software'

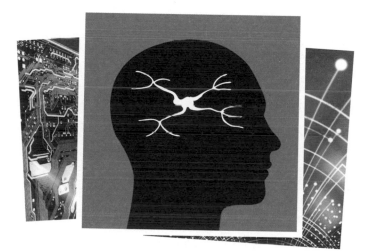

What is a Mind Map?

The human brain does not think in toolbars and menu lists; it thinks organically like all natural forms, like the human body's circulatory and nervous system, or the branches of a tree and veins in a leaf. That's how the brain thinks. To think well it needs the tool that reflects that natural organic flow. The Mind Map is that tool.

TONY BUZAN

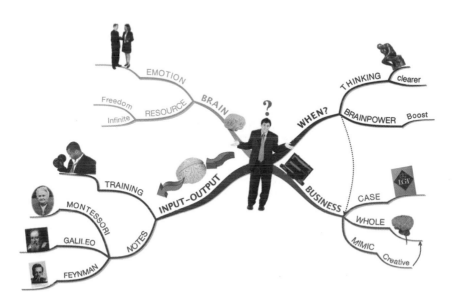

Mind Map summary for Chapter 1

How you manage your knowledge is a critical factor in creating a thriving business, and by default this comes about once you have mastered the management of your brain and its thought processes. The Mind Map is an all-embracing visual and graphic thinking tool that can harness and help you express ideas and creativity that can lead you to broaden your business practices, solve problems, rethink sales strategies, organise a team or simply improve the day-to-day efficiency of the running of your business.

The technique can be applied to all forms of thought processes – in particular to memory, creativity and learning. The Mind Map itself can be hand drawn or computer generated (more on this later) and, like the multi-functional and universally adaptable pocket knife from Switzerland, can be designed to meet any mundane or extraordinary task or problem-solving eventuality. In fact, the Mind Map has been described as 'the Swiss Army knife for the brain'.

Brain-focused business

The brain functions using multiple intelligences – not just verbal, numerical and spatial, but also kinaesthetic (bodily control), personal, social, sensual and spiritual-ethical – a skill set of intellegences first expounded by the distinguished American psychology Professor Howard Gardner of Harvard University. As we are living in the Age of Intelligence, in which multiple intelligences rule, in order to perform effectively and productively in life as well as business we need to pay heed to this and develop 'intelligent' strategies.

The Age of Intelligence has ushered in an explosive growth of brain research and an ever-increasing global fascination with the brain and its extraordinary capacities. Up until 1991, the brain had never made the front cover of any mainstream let alone business magazine, but that changed dramatically in 1991 when *Fortune*'s front cover proclaimed: 'Brainpower: how intellectual capital is becoming America's most valuable asset'. In other words, if you want to make a fortune, invest in your brain.

Over the rest of the decade and into the 'noughties', millions of articles were published on the topic. The *Far Eastern Economic Review* proclaimed: 'Wanted: brain power – labour shortage puts Asia's boom at risk'. *New Scientist* delved into the brain to reveal that the number of thoughts available to the average human brain was equal to the number of atoms in the known universe.

The need to handle the world's major source of wealth – intelligence – also convinced the *Harvard Business Review*, at the beginning of the twenty-first century, to feature 'The looming creativity crisis' on its front cover. This crisis was considered greater than the threats of trade wars and all acts of terrorism. As with the sun's energy, the crisis was (and is) not one of lack of resources; it is one of lack of *management* and *use* of an infinite resource. It is about how to use knowledge, how to store, extract, create, solve problems and think intelligently about the available data, and this is precisely what the Mind Map will help you do.

So what is a Mind Map?

In the next few chapters we will go into more detail about how to create a Mind Map yourself for various situations, but before we go on, let us explain the principle behind the original idea here.

1   A Mind Map always starts with an image at the centre – this can be something that roughly or more precisely represents the idea, concept, thought, note, theme, or subject of whatever business issue it is that you are focusing on. The subject of attention is thus crystallised in this central image.

2   From that central image, create branches that are attached to the central image and flow out in curves, not in straight lines. On these branches are placed the key concepts and these should be labelled with keywords or images. The first-level branches (or 'chapter headings') are called the Basic Ordering Ideas (BOIs).

3 From each of these BOI branches will emanate second-level branches, which will be similar in organic shape (but thinning out) and attached to each BOI branch.

4 From those branches will radiate third-level branches, extending the idea organically and naturally.

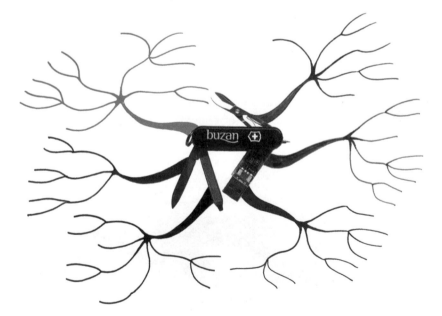

There are important rules regarding the way words and images should attach to each branch and these are dealt with in detail in Chapter 2.

When should you use Mind Maps?

You can create a Mind Map for any situation where improved learning and clearer thinking will enhance business performance. For example, brainstorming sessions or the bullet points on a presentation can be transformed into colourful, memorable, highly organised diagrams that reflect your brain's, and the brains of your audience, natural way of thinking and thus encourage synergetic thinking.

Mind Maps have an advantage in such situations, in that current information and knowledge-management techniques – chiefly standard linear note-taking – achieve the opposite effect of that desired. Linear note-taking, note-making and list-making are in fact some of the best ways in which you can destroy creativity and thinking, because they lock your brain behind 'prison bars' that methodically disconnect one thought from another. Or, worse, you find that you have started where you left off – from the bottom line in a blinkered fashion without any lateral, creative or Radiant Thinking®. The beauty (literally, as well as metaphorically) of Mind Maps is that the branches stem outwards to form another level of sub-branches that flow and dovetail with your thoughts and ideas.

Linear notes	Mind Maps
Selective	Generative
Force you to put down your best ideas and dry up your creative juices	Help you think without limitation to connect new (and more) ideas
Restrictive list	Infinite possibilities

The clue to the Mind Map's effectiveness lies in its dynamic shape and form. As the Mind Map shoots out from the centre with curved lines, symbols, words, colours and images, it reveals itself as a totally natural and organic structure. Mind Maps mimic the myriad synapses and connections of our brain cells, reflecting the way we ourselves are created and connected. Mind Maps also mimic the natural world's communication structures – witness the veins of a leaf, the branches of a tree or the blood's circulatory system.

Source: Adam Hart-Davis/Science Photo Library

So how can Mind Maps be applied to business?

Now you know what a Mind Map is all about, the next question is, what exactly can it 'do' for you in terms of your business? Do not think that a Mind Map is simply a visual aide-memoire or organised doodle: it is a dynamic and organic business tool, time manager and memory jogger that can enable you both to store and organise as well as prioritise. In addition, as you will see in the ensuing chapters, Mind Maps can be harnessed to facilitate time management, ideas generation, strategic thinking, project management, performance coaching, negotiations, risk control and other key standard business processes.

With Mind Maps you not only unlock your own amazing brainpower, but also help to stimulate the brainpower of an organisation and access quick ways to make a big impact on business.

Mind Maps to boost your brainpower

When do we stop to think about why we think and the way we think, or even the way we think about how we think? Rarely, if ever. Yet memory and learning are the building blocks of our creative thinking. We look after our bodies; what about our brains? The brain is the most important thing we can possibly train, that can make the most impact on our lives; every brain is an infinite resource that must be stimulated and developed. People often talk of the brain as a 'problem-solving organ', but in fact it is a 'solutions-finding organ'. The beauty of using Mind Maps is that they show us a very, very clear and simple way to utilise good mind skills in order to tackle all such issues.

Mind Maps: the ultimate business 'software'

LGT-Academy

One organisation that has adopted this approach is the LGT-Academy, founded by Prince Philipp of Liechtenstein, Chairman and CEO of LGT-Group, with Tony Buzan. His Serene Highness explains here how his LGT-Academy incorporates Mind Maps for open-mind training in business.

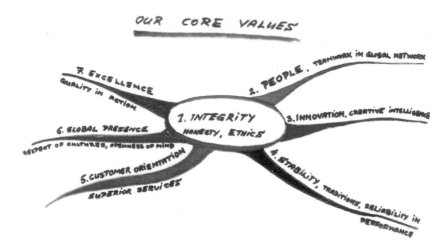

Mind Map of core values of LGT-Academy

As Chairman and CEO of LGT-Academy, I was confronted in the 1990s by the issue of how to help create an environment that would facilitate open-mindedness, as little political thinking and rivalry as possible, and not too much hierarchical behaviour. In one sentence: Have an open mind, an open door and enjoy the process of discovery.

We run an executive programme at first sight, but actually it's very different from how it appears. An executive course over a long weekend will not do! After just three to four days you will have forgotten more than 80 per cent of what you have heard and seen during such a short period. Our curriculum is therefore geared to Mind Mapping, philosophy, the arts, sports (mind sports like chess being included) and social and natural science – and we have a very high calibre of professors and coaches for the teaching.

It might sound strange to an outsider that, for a company providing financial services, specific courses in 'hard skills' such as banking, financial management and asset management very much take a back seat. We had simply decided that our aim was different: we wanted to explore the 'soft skills'. The hard-nosed businessperson may ask: Can you measure the results you achieved over the years by running this

LGT-Academy? Isn't it something of a luxury, which should be cut back sooner rather than later in the name of efficiency and cost control? Our answer is: We can understand our clients better and therefore can be of more help if we understand ourselves better, if we have learned to lead ourselves and discipline ourselves before demanding any leadership.

We have experienced over the years that our academic programme is an attraction and a plus when recruiting interesting persons or whole teams for our operations. It also, as we set out, makes building group-wide informal networks (which are independent of hierarchy, geography or function) much easier. It has helped us to have a house where doors are open. Many of us now say, 'How fascinating' when confronted with something unplanned and unexpected.

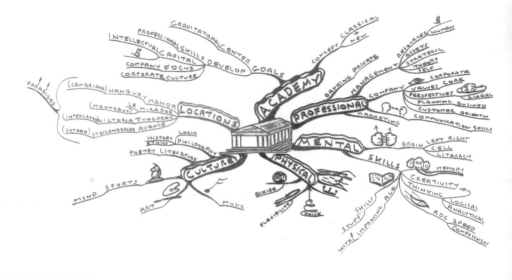

If you could see your brain 'naked' you would see not just a single remarkable object but one composed of two sides: a left hemisphere and a right hemisphere. In fact, these hemispheres lie within the cerebral cortex, the 'thinking cap', which covers 80 per cent of your brain. This is where your higher-level thinking – your use of the cognitive skills – takes place. While the left and right hemispheres of your brain have a mirrored make-up, they are home to slightly different functions. The left deals primarily with words, numbers, analysis, listing, language and logic, while the right deals with rhythm, colour, shape, maps, imagination and daydreaming.

The problem with this neat division is that it pigeonholes brainpower into 'sides'. While it may appear to be 'a brain of two halves', the two sides of

The cerebral cortex of your brain is divided into two parts: the left and right hemispheres. Each hemisphere specialises in certain processes

your brain do not work in isolation. They are linked by the *corpus callosum*, which acts as a phenomenal superconductor (with over 250 million nerve fibres) of information between the two hemispheres. The information is provided by the cognitive skills of both the left and right hemispheres.

'Whole-brain' thinking

When we ask businesspeople in our seminars, 'Where does creativity lie?' the response is invariably, 'The right side of the brain'. 'Where does business lie?' 'Left side of the brain.' 'Where do art and music lie?' 'Right side of the brain.' And so on. We then have to tell them the answer each time is: 'Wrong, wrong, wrong'. In fact, it is so dangerously wrong that if you believe this neat left or right functionality you are crippling your own and your business colleagues' intellectual capabilities.

To understand this simply, imagine yourself running a marathon, normally, with two hands and two legs.

Now imagine you are running with your left hand tied to your left foot. This is *not* equivalent to a reduction of 50 per cent of efficient arm and leg action; this represents a 99 per cent-plus dissipation of power. It is a massive drop.

Running in this way means that you spiral into negative percentages with the possibility of falling over and damaging yourself, and the same analogy applies to your business. Whether you are an individual or a corporation, if you use one side of your brain to manage knowledge, you are wasting 99 per cent of your resources and efficiency. It is not merely crippling for business, it is disastrous. You are conducting business using your brain without the gears being fully engaged – the gears being the individual elemental cognitive skills. An organisation will end up having brains that are only communicating with half their corporate skills and thinking tools until this bias creates a lopsided organisation that will eventually keel over, collapse, and crash.

Bring 'whole-brain' thinking together with a Mind Map

When used together, each side of your brain simultaneously reinforces the other in a manner that provides limitless creative potential and strengthens your ability for greater associations. This in turn leads to greater intellectual firepower.

The process of creating a Mind Map employs the entire range of cognitive skills, so in popular terms it can be seen as a 'whole-brain' thinking tool. In fact, it is *the* 'whole whole-brain thinking tool'. A Mind Map also taps into harnessing the full range of cortical skills on both the left and right hemispheres simultaneously. In this way it opens up multiple synaptic connections – true 'brainstorming' for creativity, thinking and memory.

How Mind Maps mimic the creative processes of your brain

The driving force behind your creativity is your imagination. Creativity involves going on imaginative journeys, taking yourself and your colleagues into original and previously unexplored realms. These new associations give rise to the new realisations that the world calls 'creative breakthroughs'. Mind Maps mimic the creative processes of your brain to boost ideas generation in leaps and bounds.

Your brain does not think linearly or sequentially, like a computer; it thinks multilaterally, 'radiantly'. So when you create a Mind Map, the branches grow outwards to form another level of sub-branches, encouraging you to create more ideas out of each thought you add – just as your brain does.

Because all the ideas on the Mind Map are linked to each other, your brain is able to make great leaps of understanding and imagination through association. Creativity is the development of original ideas, concepts and solutions using imagination and association – this is the premise of the Mind Map.

Intelligent input–output

A Mind Map is a natural evolutionary and quintessential process, drawing from the works of the great note-takers (Galileo Galilei, Richard Feynman and Maria Montessori, to name but a few), new theories on memory and creativity and learning, research into mnemonic (memory-enhancing) techniques, and the latest findings on the neurophysiology of the brain cell. The Mind Map – from a quick back-of-the-envelope sketch to a full-colour work of art – combines a rich history with scientific study.

The technique may not have been around for those great thinkers, but it is certainly available to business users today – both in its most simplistic form with pen and paper and even in an office-friendly, computer-generated format too. A Mind Map is the easiest way to put information into, and extract information out of, your brain – and indeed any received stimuli, by literally 'mapping out' your thoughts.

The importance of training

Any good businessperson wants to invest in a tool or piece of equipment that will grow their business and increase its profitability. They will seek a great return on investment, and yet how many entrepreneurs and organisations invest in the brain as a separate item?

Imagine you are buying hardware that allows you to, for example, calculate, communicate in multiple languages, negotiate, address and inspire thousands of individuals, or that supplies its own sources of energy and operates all other pieces of equipment in the company. How much would you pay for that hardware? It would be beyond the cost of the fastest super-computer ($US 300–400 million!). But even if you could buy it, then what? You'd have to have its operations manual, you'd have to learn how to use it so that you can program it and operate its hardware and software.

The Mind Map is just that hardware structure and software manifestation, but like the Buzan Army Knife example on page 7, you need to know how to use all of it – not just one blade, but all its applications. The following chapters in this book will show you exactly how to create hand-drawn or computer-generated Mind Maps for a wide range of business applications, while equipping you with the knowledge you need in order to use this business tool most effectively.

Free your brain

Before embarking on the 'how to', consider this: every brain in every company is an infinite resource that *must* be developed if the manager and the organisation are to achieve and maintain competitive advantage.

Our brains are wired to think with multi-sensory images and their associations and radiations, and because each individual image, concept or keyword is theoretically infinite in its ability to both radiate and associate, we should view the brain as an atomic energy device in which each individual word, image and concept is an atom of energy that has its own extraordinary nuclear power.

Confining these atoms of information and knowledge management into phrases or sentences massively reduces their energy, and in many cases totally obscures it. A Mind Map allows each atom of thought its own freedom, infinitely multiplying the possibility for thought.

Finally, imagine that each individual keyword concept is like a star that, when allowed to be free, can radiate ideas like a supernova lighting up the whole universe. If those stars are trapped in phrases and sentences they can never radiate. So, let the atoms generate! Let the stars radiate!

Source: POD/Photodisc. StockTrek

Lighting up your logic – enhancing your emotion

Does emotion have a role to play in business and thinking? Does emotion have a role to play in Mind Mapping? The answer to both these questions is yes.

Like any aspect of our behaviour, or any strength in our personalities, emotion is like a hand. Is a hand good or bad? It depends on the use. Is a computer good or bad? It depends on the use. Is the web good or bad? It depends on the use. Is emotion good or bad? It depends on the use.

The problem with emotion in business is that very often emotion is used as a weapon, an oppressive tactic, as a reason why not to do something, so negative emotions – panic, overriding fear, anger, timidity (of people in the lower echelons of the organisation who are afraid to speak up because of the stature of the boss or leader) – prevail. In addition, standard note-taking techniques tend to encourage the cementing of a negative emotion in the structure of the thinking, rather than diminishing it.

For example, in brainstorming sessions the dominant individual will lead the associated patterns of thought; the thinking will be overawed by the emotion behind it; and when the boss says something it tends to go to the top of the list of priorities. In a Mind Map the information fits where the information should reside: in the structure of ideas rather than the authority of the idea giver. The Mind Map expresses the logic of association, and pure logic is understanding the appropriate interconnectivities between different elements of information. This has nothing to do with emotion – positive or negative – and everything to do with the pure objectivity of where that information fits.

Equally, the Mind Map builds emotion, as the Mind Mapper sees how their pattern of thought is lighting pathways, making things more clear, and providing sudden realisations and 'aha' moments. A good strong emotion behind an idea can be a positive thing, driving the idea forward. It is therefore essential to use a tool which allows you to see the objective structure and to ride the emotions behind it – that is what gets team players, employees and other companies behind that vision, and that is what a Mind Map will create. That is the history of great business, great government and great leadership.

So, now that we understand the concept of a Mind Map and how it can aid creativity and the processes of your amazing brain, it's time to discover how you can create your own Mind Map for your ideas or business solutions. The next chapter will reveal how you can unleash your Radiant Thinking and capture all your creative thoughts on paper. The technique is very simple and, once learned, you will discover it is invaluable.

Listen to Tony and Chris expanding more on the qualities of the Mind Map and watch videos explaining the practical business applications for Mind Mapping at **www.MindMapsForBusiness.com**.

Mind Maps: the ultimate business 'software'

How do you create a Mind Map?

Mind Mapping is contagious because it works. It has helped businesspeople clearly perceive what was essential, discriminating it from the noise.

MASANORI KANDA, leading Japanese entrepreneur and marketeer

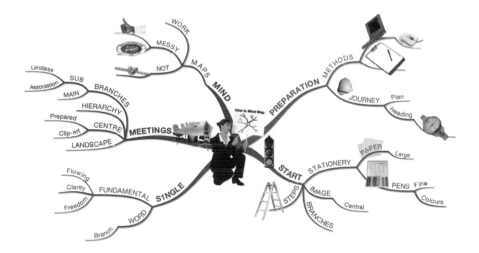

Mind Map summary for Chapter 2

There are two ways of creating a Mind Map: drawing it by hand or keying it into a computer. Whichever method you employ, first you need to decide on the topic or issue that you want to explore. Focus on the core question, the precise subject matter. Be clear about what it is that you are aiming for or trying to resolve. It is important to remember that there is no limit to what you can mind map, ranging from taking seminar notes, to preparing a speech or presentation, or simply organising the office party.

How to prepare a Mind Map

A Mind Map represents a personal thought journey on paper, and like any rewarding journey it needs some planning in order to be successful.

The first step before starting to create your mind map is to decide where you are heading. What is your goal or vision? What are the sub-goals and categories that contribute to your goal? Are you planning a specific project or are you brainstorming ideas to prepare a new strategy or product development? Do you need to take notes in a forthcoming seminar or do you just want to map out your day's tasks?

Getting started

So, once you know what it is that you want to mind map, there are a few key elements you need to organise before you begin drawing.

Stationery

If you're creating a Mind Map by hand, rather than on the computer (see Chapter 3), you will need to gather a few materials before you start.

- Use large-sized sheets of paper if you can, because you will want enough space to be able to explore your ideas. Small pages will cramp your style.

- Use a notebook or sheets of unlined paper that you can file in a ring binder, because your first Mind Map is the start of a working journal. You don't want to be inhibited subconsciously by the need to be 'neat', and you will want to keep all your ideas together in order to see how your plans and needs evolve over time. Unlined paper will allow you to free your brain to think in a non-linear, uninhibited and creative way.

- You need a good selection of easy-flowing pens with many colour options. Fine-pointed pens are particularly well suited because you will want to be able to read what you have created and you may want to write fast. Highlighters also help to keep the Mind Map vibrant and introduce structure, weight and emphasis.

- As we remember things better in colour than monochrome, it is best to use at least three colours to start networking the millions of neurons in your brain and create really strong associations and content.

Central image

The human brain finds it much easier to remember images than words, which is why in a Mind Map the central key idea and offshoot ideas are expressed as images. It is the central image that should reflect your ultimate goal.

Not all of us have learned how to draw well, and this can often be a stumbling block; but you only need to draw something representational to you, a graphic or a symbol, for example. If you are creating a Mind Map on the computer, you have the advantage of being able to use some of the many drawings, graphics and photographic images available in Clipart, either in published or electronic form. You can also copy, cut and paste an image from a magazine or the internet.

Branches

When drawing the 'branching ideas' that radiate from the central image, make the branches thick near the centre, colourful, and also equal in size to the length of the keyword or supporting image – too short and it won't fit; too long and the impact will be lost.

Print each keyword or 'hook' clearly above the branch, and in colour, to help the brain 'photograph' the word more easily to recall at a later date. Use one word per branch; each keyword represents the simplest and most obvious categories of information that will automatically attract your brain to think of the greatest number of associations.

Don't forget that you can add arrows, symbols, highlighting and other visual devices to identify the Basic Ordering Ideas and to instil hierarchy, associations and colour into your notes. Again, if you feel your drawing skills let you down, print out or copy Clipart or other pre-made images or graphics to use in your Mind Map.

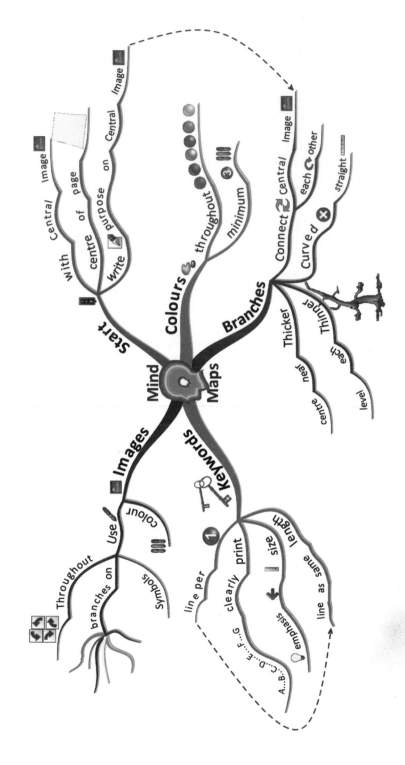

Here is a review in Mind Map form of the elements you need to create a Mind Map

Step by step to creating a Mind Map

Here is a simple exercise taken from a Japanese beginners' mind-mapping exercise class, where those attending were asked to draw a full Mind Map to develop a new stationary product. You can see the structure of ideas, imagination and creativity evolving and expanding step by step.

Step 1

Draw an image in the centre of the blank sheet of paper to represent your goal. Don't worry if you feel that you can't draw well; that doesn't matter. It is very important to use an image as the starting point for your Mind Map because it is an image that will jump-start your thinking by activating your imagination.

Step 2

Draw the first of your thick lines radiating from the centre of the image. One way to draw a main branch is to create two lines from the central image and then connect them at the tip, ready to colour in. Curve your lines rather than drawing straight ones, because drawn that way they are more interesting to your eye and therefore more memorable to your brain.

Step 3

Now colour in the main branch.

Steps 4–7

Write one keyword on each branch that you associate with the topic. These are your main thoughts (your Basic Ordering Ideas). Although it is tempting to write phrases or linked words, using only one keyword per branch allows you to define the very essence of the issue you are exploring, while also helping to store the association more emphatically in your memory. Phrases and sentences actually limit the effect and confuse your memory (see below). Add second-level or sub-branches for associated ideas and links with keywords for these as well.

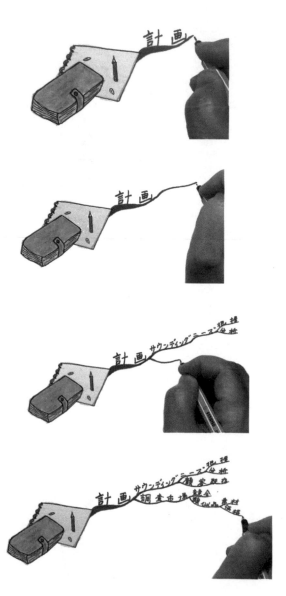

Mind Maps: the ultimate business 'software'

Step 8

In this example, the Mind Mapper is working clockwise. Create another main branch for another main theme or topic. Add a few empty branches to your Mind Map. Your brain will want to put something on them. (These two Basic Ordering Ideas are Planning and Costs.)

Step 9

Create second- and third-level branches for your related associated and secondary thoughts. The secondary level connects to the primary branches, the third level to the secondary branches, and so on. Association is everything in this process. The words that you choose for each of your branches might include themes that ask questions: the who, what, where, why, when or how of the subject or situation.

Step 10

Use images wherever possible, not just for the central idea; remember images greatly magnify your memory (a picture is worth a thousand words).

Steps 11–13

Continue the process until you have completed your hand-drawn Mind Map. In this example, the Basic Ordering Ideas are Planning, Costs, Partners, Target, Branding, Team (clockwise).

Mind Maps: the ultimate business 'software'

Why one word per branch is so essential for business Mind Mapping

As noted above, an important Mind Map guideline is that keywords need to be printed clearly above each branch and sub-branch, and only one word used per branch. Paradoxically, while appearing to restrict imaginative associations, this rule actually gives explosive freedom to the cognitive and other intelligences. The more progressively you can move from sentence thinking and phrase thinking to a single keyword thinking Mind Map, the more powerful your Mind Map will be.

It can be difficult to think of just one word to sum up your idea or thought and add it as your branch label, but it is one of the most fundamental rules of Mind Mapping; you need to do this in order to keep thought processes clear, straightforward and free flowing. The following diagrams show how the rule brings clarity to the notion of a 'missed project deadline' – at first glance a seemingly negative phrase.

Words fused together on a single branch

When two or more words are placed on a line they are naturally fused together, which means that a limit has been placed upon the direction through which the thought process can travel. So it follows that once two ideas are fused together, a certain degree of clarity is lost.

Words are on separate branches but scope is still limited

If the mind views and focuses upon only one word it can open itself up to all the possibilities this word brings forth. If, however, there are two (or more) words placed upon a branch, your brain is immediately faced with a conflict of interest: it must split its thought process and concentrate on more than one idea at once. This split breaks down the organic thought processes that are brought forth in true Mind Mapping.

In this example the key element is the 'project'. The 'deadline' is a separate issue that can be addressed and reviewed in a wider context on its own: for example, was the 'deadline' realistic in the first place? What was the timescale? What resources were allocated to it? Zooming in on the 'deadline' enables us to explore the word in relation to the business, team, project, and so on. Similarly, putting 'missed' on a separate branch enables us to drill down further into this concept. For instance, we can assess that the project was 'late' but was nevertheless 'completed' (with a tick).

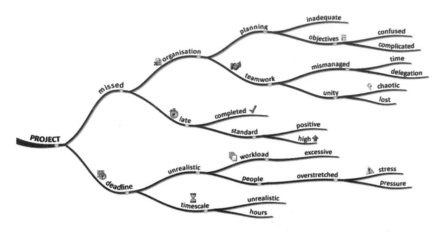

Words able to radiate by separating on single branches (organic layout)

This is not to say, however, that it is not possible to have more than one word associated with each thought. By placing just one word on each branch the Mind Mapper is able to analyse the big picture using a vast amount of smaller associations. These in turn can be analysed in great detail, giving an in-depth microscopic view of a topic without losing sight of the macroscopic.

Each word possesses a great number of possible associations – by fusing words together, you immediately limit the possible associations and in turn stifle your thought processes. By keeping the words separate clarity is maintained, which in turn helps thought processes to flow. Keeping each 'branch of thought' clear and distinct from the others also allows the user to recall this line of thought easily and without the worry of confusion. As a result the 'one word per branch' rule enhances memory and powers of recall.

It should also be restated that the 'one word' can be a single image, not forgetting that one of the other major laws of Mind Mapping is that wherever possible you should use an image. This is the best aid for recall simply because, for your brain, a picture is worth a thousand words.

Real truth and freedom of thought

In any given business scenario, for example when negotiating, adhering to the one word per branch rule will enable you to see your position far more clearly and 'truthfully', as well as the position of those with whom you are negotiating (see Chapter 5).

The truth factor can change lives. When blanket negative phrases, such as 'project deadline missed', are repeated in the memory they increasingly become the 'false truth' of that person's performance. There are many examples of people in business saying such things as 'my deadline was missed'; this is unclear, undefined and incorrect information, but if they keep thinking it they create that reality.

It is quite obvious, especially after considering the one word per branch rule, that there was more to the picture than simply the project deadline being missed, i.e. there were positive and insightful moments too. Similarly, people will say things such as 'My first business venture was a total disaster'. Again, considering the one word per branch rule, it is obvious that this is not true. The business must have had many positive aspects to it, otherwise it would never have taken off or existed in the first place.

In addition to this vitally important aspect of truth, the one word per branch Mind Map – which is a real Mind Map – gives the mind perhaps the most important gift of all: freedom. This is the freedom to express, be clear, see the whole picture, release its infinite creativity, think, remember what it wants to remember, and to explore the truly infinite universe of the mind. All are key factors in succeeding in the business world.

With all these advantages, the one word per branch Mind Map also has another wonderful by-product – the reduction of stress. As stress is one of the business world's biggest problems, the one word per branch Mind Map can be seen as a health remedy.

Planning a meeting: how to prepare a Mind Map, step by step

The following steps outline a typical business application to get you started. If you are not sure what your BOIs should be, ask yourself the following simple questions with regard to your main goal or vision:

- What knowledge is required in order to achieve my aim?

- If this were a book, what would the chapter headings be?

- What are my specific objectives?

- What are the seven most important categories in this subject area?

- What are the answers to my seven basic questions: Why? What? Where? Who? How? Which? When?

- Is there a larger, more encompassing category that all of these fit into that it would be more appropriate to use?

Step 1

Turn your first sheet of paper sideways in front of you (landscape-style) in order to start your Mind Map in the centre of the page. This will allow you freedom of expression without being restricted by the narrow measure of the page. Create your image or use Clipart or other prepared images.

Using this Mind Map example of running a meeting you may ask 'Where is it going to be held?', 'What are the objectives?', 'Who should attend?', and so on. Therefore you may decide on elements such as 'location', 'agenda', 'objectives' as appropriate keyword labels for your first branches.

Step 2

There is a hierarchy to the structure of the Mind Map, with the most important elements being located closer to the central image. Write one keyword that you associate with planning your meeting on each branch in bold colourful capitals. For example, 'when', 'who', 'agenda', 'location', 'supplies', 'objectives'. These are your main thoughts (and your Basic Ordering Ideas).

Step 3

You can use association to expand your Mind Map to the final stage. Look at the keywords on the main branches to achieve this. These keywords should spark off further ideas. Draw smaller branches that stem from the keywords to accommodate the associations you make. Add your sub-branches to your first main branch. For example, to 'agenda' add 'previous', 'minutes', 'actions', 'AOB'. You can also add a few empty branches to your Mind Map. Your brain will want to put something on them. Numbers for hierarchy are very helpful prompts too.

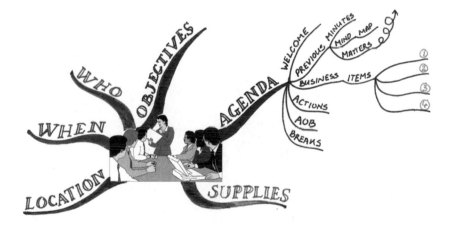

Step 4

The number of sub-branches is potentially limitless, dependent only upon the number of ideas that you can think of. For example, the sub-branches of 'supplies' may be 'food', 'drink', 'materials' and 'pens'.

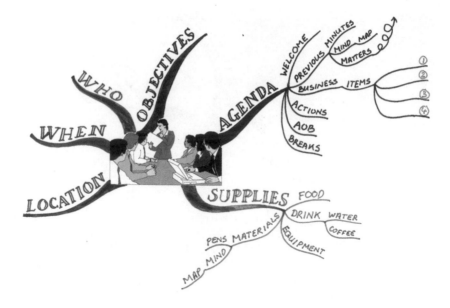

Step 5

The sub-branch may then trigger more thoughts and ideas associated with the keyword of that branch, leading to the development of the next level of sub-branches. Continuing clockwise, add the next set of sub-branches. For example, to 'location' add 'book', 'room'.

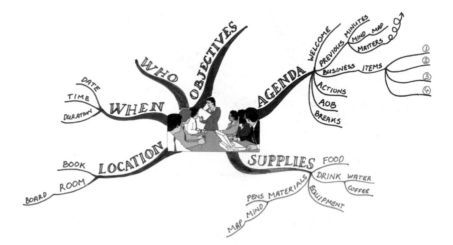

Step 6

Continue this process of adding sub-branches until all your thoughts and ideas are on your Mind Map.

It's important to distinguish a 'true' Mind Map from a 'proto' Mind Map. Take a look at the following examples; they represent proto-Mind Maps drawn or created by those who haven't quite grasped the basics.

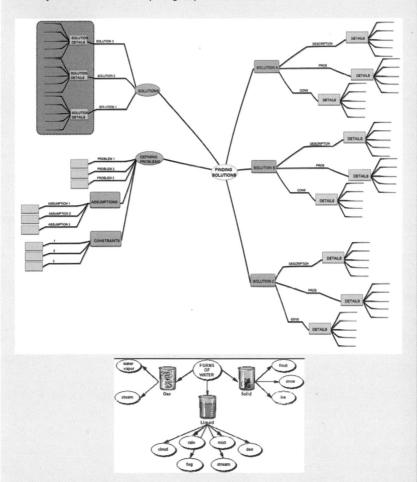

Examples of non Mind Maps

At first glance they may seem acceptable, but in fact they ignore the key principles of Mind Mapping. Each idea is on its own, cut off from the others. There is no dynamic connection between the branches and nothing to encourage your brain to spark with new ideas. They are designed to cut off thought. Using phrases instead of single words also hinders associations and imagination. Compare this with the outline of a Mind Map that closely follows all the important principles on page 32.

When a messy Mind Map is a good Mind Map

It's also fair to point out that there may be occasions when and where you simply can't adhere to all the key elements that make up a true Mind Map. For example, in a small huddled meeting or when you suddenly have brainstorming ideas but no set of coloured pens or A4 pad on which to record them. In these circumstances it's perfectly reasonable to jot down a Mind Map on the back of an envelope, beer mat, torn piece of lined paper, pocket notebook, or whatever is to hand using any writing implement you can lay your hands on. That's fine. Some of the most creative ideas have been launched that way.

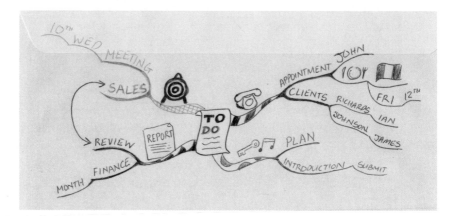

So if you simply need to Mind Map a 'to do' list' quickly, say, in a coffee bar, it will be a result of that organic situation and will be an accurate reflection of your state of mind at the time. However 'messy' the Mind Map is, it is still likely to contain more information of value than would have been the case had you simply noted everything down in a list.

You can copy or expand on your Mind Map when you get back to the office or after the meeting; indeed, you *should* try to take some time to transform your Mind Map notes into a more finished version. However, even with these limitations your Mind Map is still infinitely better than a list or set of bullet points. You can copy and colour it in when you get back to your desk, or you can transfer it to a computer (see Chapter 3 and visit **www.imindmap.com/tutorials**, which has a dedicated tutorial on how to create an iMindMap).

Taking Mind Maps to your work

Once you have grasped the fundamental rules of Mind Mapping outlined in this chapter, you are ready to try out a Mind Map, perhaps by copying the examples given here using pens and paper. Be prepared for some trial and error; it won't necessarily 'click' first time, especially with the drawing aspects. Endure the 'perspiration' to get the 'inspiration' and you will find that Mind Maps revolutionise how you capture, store and disseminate business information, insight and ideas.

If you prefer to work on computer and communicate with others via technological means, the next chapter will introduce you to a whole new world of Mind Mapping using iMindMap software.

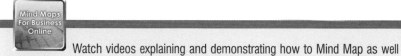

Watch videos explaining and demonstrating how to Mind Map as well as tutorials, tips, iMindMap templates and how-to guides at **www.MindMapsFor Business.com**.

Mind Mapping on a computer

I use Mind Maps in every area of my life, especially business – I used them to help develop one of Europe's fastest-growing technology companies – but I wanted to use them on a computer and I wanted to be able to mind map on a computer with the freedom that I can on paper. I was able to work with Tony Buzan to realise a dream to produce the world's first Mind Map software that fully duplicates the non-linear thinking process of the human brain.

CHRIS GRIFFITHS

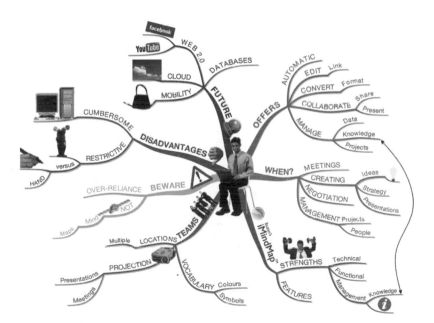

Mind Map summary for Chapter 3

In this computer-dominated age there is a real demand for software that enables mind maps to be created on screen rather than on paper. For businesses and individuals who prefer to work this way, the good news is that computers can now replicate the dynamic creativity of colourful, hand-drawn Mind Maps – but with a whole host of added features that make them adaptable, updatable, and also gives the user the ability to share them with colleagues and integrate the program with other standard business software processes.

Computer Mind Maps have really come of age, with features and functions dedicated to easy business use, especially with the advent of iMindMap (see page 41). But hand-drawn Mind Maps will continue to be the first port of call where personal–physical contact, aesthetic movement, more comprehensive memory and more immediate creativity are required. Moreover there are some situations – where space for a laptop is restricted, computers are not available and time is limited, or the order of ideas for a meeting is not immediately apparent – in which a Mind Map sketched on a 'back of an envelope' may still be the most pragmatic solution.

The other key advantage of a hand-drawn Mind Map is that it has the 'fingerprint' of the maker's brain; the complex electroencephalograms expressed as words and images. It is distinguishable by its very style, the unique style of that 'artist'. The Mind Map also activates the different areas of your brain: visual, kinesthetic, tactile, rhythmic, colour – in other words it becomes multi-sensory, especially when *you* are drawing it. It is itself a massive spark for the creativity process. It is also wholly organic, requiring no interface or digital transfer to get your thought into a Mind Map.

For analysing, communicating, leading, problem-solving, creating, remembering and thinking objectively, the hand-drawn Mind Map will continue to be the springboard for creativity. Having said that, the computer Mind Map opens up amazing applicability and flexibility in the business environment.

Businesses – from sole traders to global organisations – need to share information with colleagues, clients and any other interested parties, and they can do this electronically via email using attachments, through websites, presentations, reports, memos and a host of other standard software processes.

Traditionally, hand-drawn Mind Maps were not ideal for sharing and disseminating in the business environment, although they could be copied. Even with the advent of computer Mind Mapping, computer-generated Mind Maps initially remained cumbersome, diagrammatic and not 'fit for purpose' – indeed, not offering much more than an extended flowchart. Computer Mind Mapping is now being reworked to correct these fundamental flaws and be more useful to a wider spectrum of business needs and requirements.

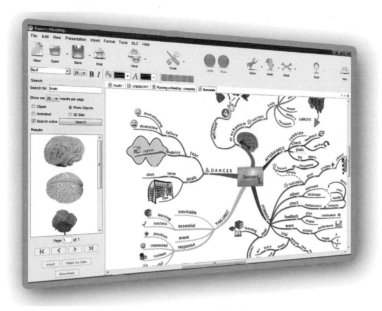

A computer-generated Mind Map created using iMindMap software

What does computer Mind Mapping offer?

Although computers are still some way from reproducing the organic and interconnected nature of real human thought, mind mapping software has made real progress in being able to duplicate the visual variety, fluidity and portability that is offered by traditional pen and paper Mind Mapping.

In general, computer mind-mapping software today offers many enhanced features to help boost your mental processes and productivity. There are many stand-alone software programs available as well as web-based applications, several of which will allow you to do the following:

- automatically generate neat and colourful Mind Maps quickly and with little effort;

- edit and enhance your Mind Maps as much as you like;

- analyse and manage your data at intricate levels using a range of tools;

- share and present your Mind Maps through a variety of modes;

- convert your Mind Maps into different communication and reporting formats, such as reports, presentations, project plans and spreadsheets;

- leverage group ideas and comments through collaboration;

- organise, implement and track projects from start to finish;

- improve knowledge management through links to external information sources.

Computer Mind Mapping – when to use it

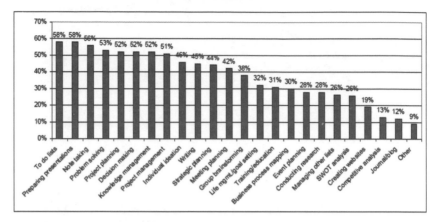

Mind Mapper Chuck Frey conducted a survey on his weblog to find out how popular Mind Maps were among business users. The results are shown here

Source: Chuck Frey, **www.mindmappingsoftwareblog.com**

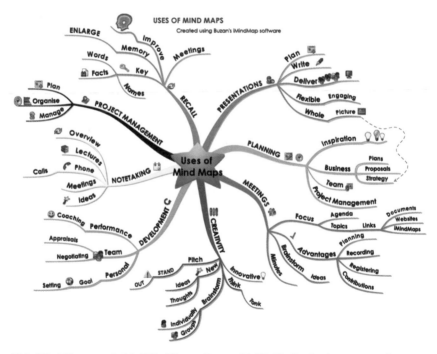

This Mind Map, created in iMindMap software, highlights the business uses of Mind Mapping

As you will discover in the following chapters of this book, computer Mind Mapping is the ultimate utility tool for a wide range of business applications, but it is particularly effective when used in meetings, for brainstorming, negotiation, strategy development, project management and also in presentations, speeches, lectures and performance appraisals (See figure opposite).

Introducing iMindMap

Tony Buzan originated Mind Maps with pen and paper, but for years he has recognised the huge advantages of being able to transfer his invention to computer to give this technique a place in today's modern, technological world. He says, 'Ever since I invented Mind Maps I've dreamed of the day when the computer would be able up to catch up with the human brain, because up to now it couldn't: it was too restricted, too rigid, too dull ... fundamentally computers couldn't mind map. What was needed was the freedom, the extraordinary variety, the visual beauty, the organic nature of the way that the human mind actually thinks. It had been tried a number of times and very, very seriously failed. Many people tried but what came out were proto-Mind Maps, poor imitations, more robotic, linear, truncated, and they didn't allow the brain to expand.'

So, in 2005, Chris Griffiths and Tony Buzan teamed up to produce iMindMap – finally creating a software that reflects the brain's true organic nature and mimics how our brains' thought processes interact.

It was a challenging process that required pulling together a team of experts in different fields of technology and software from around the world. Having been a product sold exclusively via the internet, in February 2008 iMindMap was launched in-store in Japan for the first time. It reached the No. 1 slot in Amazon Japan as its best-selling software product above computer games, anti-virus offerings, office utilities and learning tools.

Special software allows this powerful and flexible business thinking tool to be moved around the organisation via email, taken into meetings and brainstorming sessions, displayed on projectors and migrated into other leading office software. It quite simply transfers the thoughts you are thinking visually and directly onto a computer screen, and crucially will help to improve the dynamic of the people, the teams and the organisation as a whole by creating a better thinking environment and better organisational thinking skills. (For more information, visit **www.imindmap.com**.)

The strengths of true mind-mapping software

The advantages of Mind Mapping on computer go beyond the purely technical benefits; by their very nature and the scope of information technology, iMindMaps can be used to communicate ideas and information to colleagues and clients with great effectiveness.

Technical

The technical pros for creating Mind Maps on the computer come down to their editability in being able to change colour, shrink or expand branches; as well as the ease with which they can be enhanced by importing graphics, video or audio, can include hyperlinks to spreadsheets, documents, media, websites, or can be linked to produce multi-level maps. The software also enables various modes of collaboration to support brainstorming, presentation, project planning, research and makes the created Mind Maps compatible, convertible and exportable to other formats.

Functional

Computer-generated Mind Maps are infinitely flexible, more so than paper-generated ones, allowing the user to capture ideas very quickly, for example in speed mind-mapping mode. The software also possesses idea-filtering features, can generate reports based on the information it includes, and enables different presentation modes, such as MS PPT or website.

Knowledge and information management

Through the miracle of modern technology and its information highways, iMindMaps connect people to information in a direct, effective way. Sharing data and ideas via email, internal computer systems and via websites means that information is better managed, avoiding duplication, and can be easily synchronised or synthesised with other data.

Key features in true computer Mind Mapping

There are several advantages to computer-generated Mind Maps that hand-drawn Mind Maps cannot share, and so inevitably this method does extend the technique of Mind Mapping beyond its traditional capabilities, even without special add-on features.

iMindMap (for which we developed and launched the latest version in 2009) adheres to the rules and brain-friendly concepts of true Mind Maps as outlined in Chapter 2, with the additional benefits of computer technology when it comes to being able to create instantly legible ideas that can be swiftly and easily copied and shared across teams and departments.

Automatic Mind Map generation

Creating a computer Mind Map is extremely simple and intuitive when using modern software applications; there are absolutely no space limitations – you

Mind Maps: the ultimate business 'software'

will not reach the edge of your workspace as you would when Mind Mapping on paper, because you can simply continue to scroll across the screen.

Digital ink

A further exciting option for automatically generating your Mind Maps involves 'digital ink'. If you like being able to hand-draw your Mind Maps but recognise the advantages of creating them via the computer, this technique offers a good compromise. You can hand-draw your computer Mind Maps directly onto the screen of a tablet PC or interactive whiteboard using a digital pen, just as if you were using conventional pen and paper.

Unrestricted restructuring and editing

Once you have created your Mind Map, you can easily 'flex' and restructure it to make it more meaningful, to accommodate new insights and ideas or reflect changing circumstances or priorities, or to manipulate the information you require to see. For example, as the need arises you can add, remove, or move around branches of keywords in seconds at the click of the mouse in order to clearly rearrange and reorganise your thoughts and ideas, without covering the page with crossings out and other marks.

Thus when it comes to giving a professional-looking presentation, a computer-generated Mind Map often has the advantage over a hand-drawn one in that it is clear and legible. It is also easy to attach notes, documents and links to branches and ideas. The software also allows total flexibility in shifting and transforming the shape, length, curvature and direction of any branch, and allows you to change quickly the colour of any branch, word or image as you go along and as your ideas develop. You can arrange and rearrange your topics until your Mind Map perfectly represents your ideas. This is virtually impossible to do in a hand-drawn Mind Map without redrawing it several times.

Importing and editing

iMindMaps also have aesthetic advantages over pen and paper; if drawing is not your strong point, you can use the program to illustrate your Mind Map simply by importing one of a vast library of images.

Many software programs also allow you to import, save and edit pre-existing Mind Maps from other mind-mapping applications. This saves you valuable time when reproducing Mind Maps and enables you to use your preferred software program for customisation.

Improved analysis and management of information

Computer Mind Maps allow you to include much more information than could be reasonably managed in a physical drawing. Indeed, your computer Mind Map is easily transformed into a serious knowledge management tool, which is perfect for handling information overload and breaking down important details for in-depth analysis.

'Big picture' to minute detail navigation

Your Mind Map is no longer limited by the size of paper that you use, it is only limited by your imagination – and that is infinite. An essential feature of computer Mind Mapping is therefore the ability to explore and navigate through the organic pathways of the Mind Maps. You need to know where you are, always remain in control, and have the ability to view specific areas. With computer Mind Maps you can take a helicopter view of your Mind Map, exploring vertically and horizontally within the Mind Map hierarchy without getting lost. This is not just seeing 'the wood for the trees', it is getting an 'aerial' view of the whole Amazon rainforest while simultaneously zooming into a single jungle hardwood tree, then on to the leaf and vine, and then on to the veins of the leaf and beyond into the chemical molecules of the leaf, and so on *ad infinitum*.

Navigating computer Mind Maps (combined with branch expand and collapse options) allows you to see as much or as little detail as you require. For example, in a presentation you can project the Mind Map onto a screen and zoom in temporarily to focus in on one branch, turning the selected branch into the central theme of a new Mind Map. Allowing branches to be hidden or highlighted, and without the distractions of your original Mind Map, you can look at ideas and information at a more objective level and really concentrate on the new topic, helping the team to maintain focus. Presenting a problem or subject for discussion in this way helps colleagues to evolve their own ideas and thought structures.

Instant access

Often in negotiations or discussions you will find that you need information quickly in order to reinforce a point, and to this end iMindMap software allows you to search the contents of your Mind Map or multiple Mind Maps for keywords or phrases. By changing the focus of your Mind Map to the searched content, this function can also help you question and analyse your Mind Map more effectively and give you more meaningful insight into its content. This also means, in effect, that you are no longer constrained by the size of your computer screen and you do not need to have your Mind Map spread over a number of pages or files.

Transferring knowledge

iMindMaps can evolve over time, too; you can save the document and revisit it later as inspiration strikes or when new research, figures or information alter your ideas. You can add notes to any branch of your Mind Map using a 'Notes Editor', which also enables you to drill down from a secondary branch, whose ideas you wish to explore further or focus on, to create a new Mind Map with a new central image. (Drilling down beyond one word per branch is a rule that is intended to inspire new avenues of thought. See Chapter 2 for further explanation.)

You can also attach attributes such as documents, websites, URLs, applications, other Mind Maps and folders on your computer to any branch. There is no limit to the number of links you can add to a branch, helping you collate information from a variety of sources for improved understanding. You just click for fast access to all your supporting information!

Presenting knowledge

A powerful advantage of mind-mapping software is that you can employ it as an active tool for presentations, something that is harder to do with a hand-drawn Mind Map.

An example of how iMindMap software can be used in presentations

There are various ways in which you can deliver impressive and lively presentations using software:

Expand branches one by one

By collapsing all branches of your Mind Map initially, you can go through your presentation expanding branches one level at a time. Exposing the contents of your Mind Map incrementally keeps your audience focused on the topic at hand and allows you to control how much information is revealed at any one time, thereby not overwhelming your audience.

Interactive Mind Map presentations

This enables you to present with an interactive Mind Map. You can zoom in and out of branches, link direct to any files, websites or other Mind Maps during the presentation itself. This method really brings your Mind Map to life and will captivate your audience.

Focus on specific topics

Using 'Focus in' and 'Focus out' tools, you can temporarily zoom in on one particular branch of your Mind Map, turning it into a new central idea. This is great for encouraging audience participation as you can add their thoughts and ideas to new branches linked to your focused topic.

Ensure your material is readily available

Once created, computer-generated Mind Maps can be exported into other mainstream office software such as Microsoft Office and OpenOffice.Org in formats that can open up the project to group collaboration. Changing their format also means that Mind Maps can be shared electronically via the web or email for the audience to access after your presentation. You can easily attach additional information to the branches such as files or web links to help your audience follow up the information they are interested in. Or, for less computer-literate colleagues or clients, you could offer printouts of the finished Mind Map.

Converting to conventional forms of communication and reporting

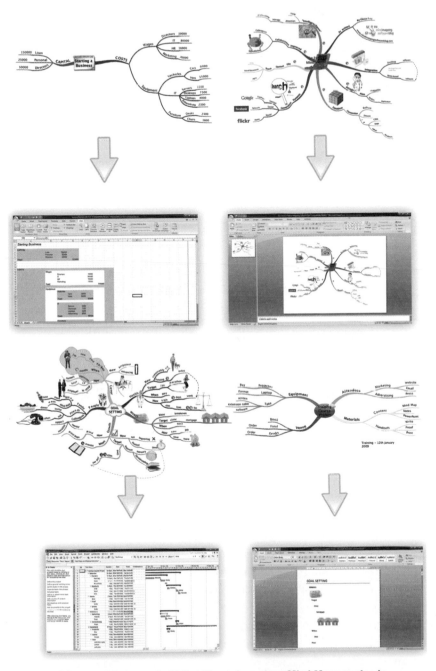

This set of 4 computer-generated Mind Maps shows how Mind Maps evolve in different computer programs

In the modern business world you might face 'cultural' barriers to presenting your colleagues or manager with coloured paper drawings of your plans or updates. Business decisions tend to be based on computer reports, proposals, presentations and project plans, so, at the click of a button, you can export your ideas as Mind Maps into Word documents, PowerPoint presentations, spreadsheets and Microsoft Project plans for all to see. This is a great time saver when your colleagues, managers or clients demand a document, spreadsheet, presentation or project plan from you; you won't need to put in hours of additional labour because the software will do the work for you.

For example, using the following export options in the iMindMap software you can convert your Mind Maps:

- **Text document** – Export your Mind Map as a formatted text outline in Microsoft Word or OpenOffice Writer.

- **Spreadsheet** – If you have a Mind Map containing financial projections, costings, sales reports or other financial data, you can export it as a spreadsheet in Microsoft Excel or OpenOffice Calc.

- **Presentation** – You can export your Mind Map as a standard 'slideshow' presentation or animated one-slide Mind Map presentation to applications like Microsoft PowerPoint, OpenOffice Impress or Mac Keynote.

- **Project plans** – Export your project Mind Maps to Microsoft Project where you can perform advanced project analysis using the application's features.

The ability to export information in this way is an immensely powerful benefit to business – it is the starting place from which to form and structure ideas for a variety of creative and communicative tasks.

Sharing

It is important that knowledge is shared in business, and what better way than to be able to make your Mind Maps quickly available to other people?

You can do this in a number of ways depending on your colleagues' requirements, computer literacy and whether you want them to have the information to hand before, during, or after a meeting. If you want to provide hard-copy Mind Maps you can print them off in a variety of formats such as single or multiple pages, in colour or in black and white, with headers or without, as a text outline, etc.

If you want to file your Mind Maps on your computer or disk to revisit later, or if you want to post them onto a website for others to view, you can export a copy of your Mind Map as an image file (JPEG, bitmap, etc.) and even choose the quality of your image. The scalable vector graphics (SVG) option

Mind Maps: the ultimate business 'software'

is ideal if you want to export your Mind Map as a high-quality graphic, which can be used in posters or books, in packages such as Adobe Illustrator, or posted on the web. Alternatively, you can export your Mind Map as an Adobe PDF file which creates a read-only version of your Mind Map, along with links and notes that others can view easily. The PDF file format is the universal standard for electronic document distribution worldwide.

Mind Mapping with teams

Groups of people stimulate and inspire each other to create ideas by thinking together, feeding off each other's diverse experiences and harnessing their collective imaginative brainpower. So how can you make this sort of 'creative huddle' around a Mind Map on a computer?

Presentations and meetings are obvious situations where this can happen, as Mind Maps can be projected onto a large screen and everyone can work on them together. This is a productive method for team meetings or group brainstorming sessions. Seeing ideas and information recorded 'live' within the context of the session gives the computer Mind Map a degree of potency that cannot be matched using flipcharts and coloured pens.

While many Mind Maps are generated by individuals, each often works as part of a team or organisational structure, but if you can't get everybody together in one room, how can you best communicate your ideas or open up a discussion about them? Perhaps the content of your Mind Map has to go through an approval cycle before its solutions or ideas can be acted upon, or perhaps you have the beginnings of an idea and want to circulate it to others to get them to offer their input and help to flesh it out? Whatever your purpose, the joy of computer technology is that it can enable group collaboration by making it possible for people in different locations to work together on the same Mind Map. Emailing a Mind Map that you've created for their review, or uploading it to a shared workspace will allow key people and other team members to contribute their ideas or give feedback on it. Each contributor can mark comments with special identifying attributes so that when the Mind Maps are returned to you each person's input can be extracted and merged into one computer 'super' Mind Map.

For ongoing projects it is a good idea to establish a visual vocabulary that defines the standard use of symbols, colours and styles for maps that are shared. By developing a shared understanding of what they mean with your team members you can then use these visual enhancements consistently.

If others are involved in the active development of the computer Mind Map they are more likely to understand the benefits of undertaking key strategies and to be enthusiastic about implementing certain tasks. (Mind Mapping with teams is further explored in Chapters 4 and 7.)

Beware electronic non Mind Maps

If you Google mind-mapping software it will show up hundreds of different tools – from generic products to niche market resources for project management and ideas generation – but web-based mapping tools have limited functions and after initial interaction are ultimately disappointing. It might claim to be a Mind Map tool, but is it really? Does it follow the rules?

Avoid these non Mind Maps as they do not engage both sides of your brain and do not allow that creative 'spark' and crossover between left and right hemispheres (see page 13) to light up or leap over. They may be labelled and publicised as 'Mind Maps', but they are not; and so should be avoided.

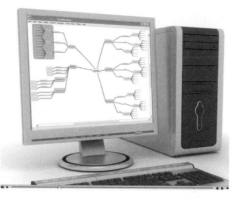

Example of a non Mind Map

The key differences between such concept maps and Mind Maps are outlined in the table below.

Concept maps v Mind Maps

Concept maps	Mind Maps
Many 'main ideas'	One focused idea
Many words in one box	Only one word per branch
Lines are not hierarchical, hence less structure	Lines are related in terms of hierarchy
Lines are not necessarily connected	Line *must* be connected
Lines are not differentiated	Lines go from thick to thin
Colours are optional	Colours are *very* important
Images are optional	Images are *very* important

Mind Maps: the ultimate business 'software'

A brilliant software tool if used properly

As we have seen – and will see throughout the rest of this book – computer Mind Maps are amazingly flexible: the number of different things you can do with them, from a business standpoint, start with its application as a white-space thinking tool. With computer Mind Maps you can plan a meeting, develop a business plan, manage a project, plan a report, track your personal goals, create a database of ideas, create lists of tasks and track your progress on them, and much more. Of course you can also do many of the same things as you can with hand-drawn maps, but not to the level of detail (or with the collection of related, linked resources and files) that is possible with mind-mapping software.

However, we must also remember that the impact of computers on working lives has a negative as well as positive side. After all, software is created by software operatives, not business users, and the over-reliance on computers, from switching on in the morning to shutting down at night, can end up forcing you to think strictly within the confines of the software you're using. This is why, in this fiercely technological age, it is even more important that you use the full set of your cognitive skills when debating issues or trying to find solutions in business. That way you avoid narrowing your vision.

Hand-drawn versus computer Mind Maps

Despite their numerous functional benefits and rapidly developing ability to duplicate the fluidity of organic Mind Mapping, it is true that hand-drawn Mind Maps have some advantages over those that are computer-generated.

The most obvious disadvantages of the technological versions come into play in situations where there is no immediate access to computers; where time is limited; or the order of ideas of a meeting is not immediately apparent. In those circumstances a Mind Map sketched on the 'back of an envelope' may still be the most pragmatic solution. There are also other situations in which getting back to basics with pen and paper may be the most effective method of creating a Mind Map.

Structure and formatting

Computer Mind Maps cannot entirely compete with the creative possibilities of organically formed Mind Maps, particularly when you want to create your own personal work of art to help you associate and recall things in a highly individualised way. Hand-drawn Mind Maps involve far greater personal input from you, making them a powerful learning device.

Some computer Mind Map packages pose a few restrictions on layout and formatting; for example, many programs limit you to only one central theme. Also, it is tempting to use default computer settings for branches, colours, fonts or layout, resulting in a Mind Map that is less individual, less visually stimulating and hence less memorable than an organically formed version. What's more, easy access to Clipart, photos and other types of images within the software means that you are less likely to add your own personal drawings that convey your exact thoughts and ideas, resulting in a Mind Map that is less unique than one drawn by hand.

Cumbersome computers

On occasions when you need to be really inventive, using a computer can be unwieldy and may stifle the creative process by decreasing spontaneity of thought. For instance, if you have to wait to put your computer on and load up a software package, you can lose vital creative time and forget important ideas. In these cases, using highly portable and accessible pen and paper tools to sketch out a Mind Map quickly prevents you losing your creative flow. However, once you've got your ideas down on paper you can always use a software program to tidy up your hand-drawn Mind Map and enhance it later.

Over-reliance on software

Another downside is the effect of increasing over-reliance on screen-based interactions on the functioning of the human brain. If we sit at our desks randomly clicking on icons and menu options, reacting to emails and the like, in the long run our brains can become lazy. This is even more apparent if a computer suddenly crashes.

The future of Mind Maps

The programmers and developers of iMindMap recognise the importance of interaction between software and user, so they are continuing to improve the interaction of the software with the organic and radiating way in which the brain cell functions. With developments in technology and methods of communicating expanding and opening up new possibilities every day, this software, like any other computer software relied upon by businesses and individuals alike, has to be revisited and improved to keep pace with the changing times.

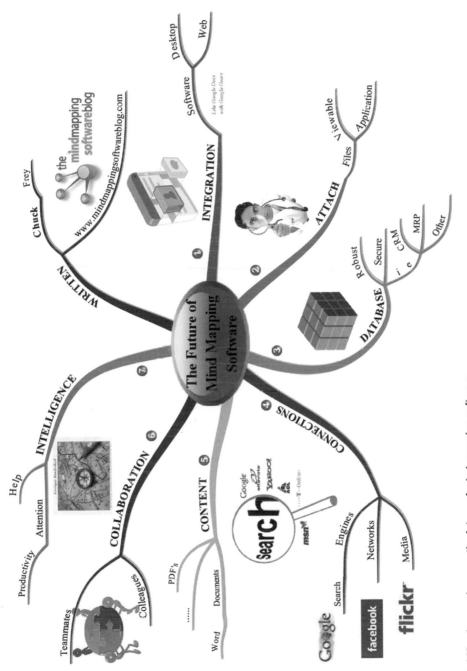

This Mind Map image shows us the future of mind-mapping software

Mobility

Until we can carry our computers around with us all the time, in our pocket or handbag, we won't always be able to use them for Mind Mapping. However, hand-held computers and mobile phones are becoming increasingly powerful and economic, and can support the running of mind-mapping software. We can also look forward to 'hands-free' Mind Mapping, with the latest developments in software support integration with voice-recognition technology.

Cloud computing

'Cloud computing' is the facility to access a cloud of online resources. Many software packages are based around a desktop mind-mapping experience, but with the increasing prominence and accessibility of the internet, the future will see more of a convergence between web-based and desktop applications. For instance, as well as being able to conduct web searches and online database queries from within desktop software, you will also be able to access and edit your Mind Maps from anywhere via a combination of desktop and web-based applications.

Stronger database connections

Mind-mapping software will be able to connect, via proper security protocols, to corporate databases such customer relationship management (CRM) and material requirements planning (MRP) systems, enabling you to seamlessly search for and extract relevant data for use in your Mind Maps. This is an especially valuable feature for complex project Mind Maps that consolidate a wealth of information.

Web 2.0 connections

Mind-mapping software will be able to interact with next generation Web 2.0 tools such as social networking (Facebook, etc.), blogging and user-generated video (YouTube), which will help to encourage mass participation and collaboration, helping people communicate.

Taking Mind Maps into the office

With an understanding of how both hand-drawn and computer Mind Mapping reflect the way your brain works naturally, and how the process of creating Mind Maps reinforces your learning and boosts your memory, you can now apply Mind Maps to a range of specific business scenarios. Chapter 4 starts with a business scene that everyone can relate to: how can I improve my time management and be more productive – notably learning how to 'map' out the working day, week and month, plan meetings and take notes more efficiently.

 Check out Tony and Chris explaining the history of Mind Mapping on a computer and the evolution of iMindMap at www.MindMapsForBusiness.com. You will also find iMindMaps articles, tutorials, tips and templates.

iMindMap is one of the most **useful organisational tools** that I use on a daily basis. I use it whenever I want to **gather my thoughts** – from training sessions to managing projects. When I use it in **meetings or presentations**, people have commented on how the topics were **easier to understand**. iMindMap is an **invaluable tool** in helping me succeed at work.

Neil Quiogue, Information Security, PopCap Games International

Part 2
Mind Mapping for core business skills

Managing yourself in time and being better organised

Eighty per cent of our corporate documentation and internal messaging is now in Mind Maps. We achieve far greater clarity in all our communication, develop more creative ideas faster and save volumes of time daily using Mind Maps. In essence – we get more done.

CLIFF SHAFFRAN, CEO, Q3global

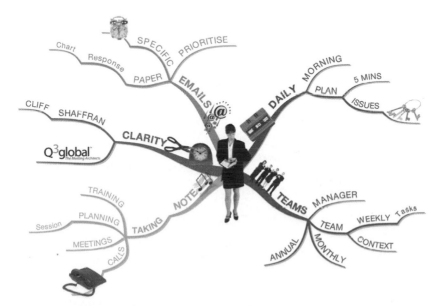

Mind Map summary for Chapter 4

You rush into the office and realise you've got so much information from so many different angles and so many things to prioritise – two proposals to write, a spreadsheet on marketing to finish, three meetings to organise – you don't know where to start. There simply isn't enough time in the day to achieve half of what you need to get done. Does this sound familiar? Here is one of the simplest but most effective ways of using a Mind Map: planning your day and allocating tasks, deadlines and priorities. Make it a daily part of your schedule.

Mind map your business day

Beginning each morning by drawing a five-minute Mind Map about the day ahead will give you a good start and save you much wasted time later on when you try to decide what to do next. A Mind Map marked up with your 'to do' list allows you to view and review your tasks – what you need to prioritise according to deadlines, and what you can realistically achieve against what is not achievable or viable in the timescale.

Seeing it all laid out also helps you get a picture of what is the 'fluff' (the fuzzy stuff you can spend ages doing but is not actually going to make much impact), and what are the key issues that need addressing and the work that needs to be done in order to achieve the result you want. Identify these and you can also pinpoint the key steps, key people and contacts you need to engage with to make it happen.

When you get to the end of the day you can then look back at your Mind Map and, with satisfaction, see what you've actually achieved, ticking off the relevant branches. This will inspire you and motivate you to do it all again the next day, as it becomes an essential tool for efficiency at work.

As discussed in the previous chapters, you can hand draw your Mind Map or create a template on iMindMap, whichever method suits you best.

1 Using a Mind Map, make your day your central image.

2 Add the main parts of the day as key branches; alternatively, you can make each main branch a major word item you want to accomplish that day.

3 From these main branches draw sub-branches with names, events or other codes to visualise what needs to be done to make each task happen.

4 Look at each step to see what's linked to it.

From your central image of tasks you can create branches for different periods of the day, or people you need to contact, or specific tasks that need to be done today, on other deadlines, or whatever other criteria work for you. As the Mind Map builds up, the beauty of it is that you see your workload objectively – what's important and what's not – and create more associations.

When you complete each task (branch and sub-branch), rather than scrawl or cross them out, mark them with a coloured tick. If you use a cross you are crossing out the task, negating it, which gives the wrong signal. A tick at the end of the branch is a confirmation – a 'job done' – and tremendously motivating. It's a positive reinforcement and affirmation of your progress through the working day.

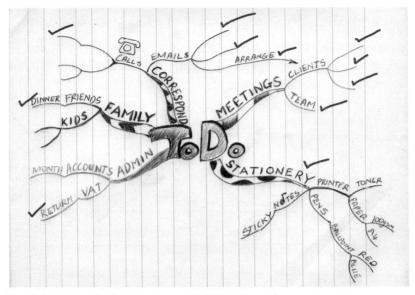

A hand-drawn sketch showing a completed Mind Map

Organising your day with Mind Map plans and tasks

Getting an overview of things to do day-to-day is quite challenging when you use linear notes. Your brain is an extraordinary associative machine: it allows thoughts to pop into your head, sometimes without apparent logic. Taking these thoughts down in a list and trying to structure them at the same time is virtually impossible. You end up with a mass of scribbled notes between lines or even forget to mark things down because they didn't fit.

Mind Maps, on the other hand, allow you to 'zap' and 'stay structured' at the same time. Mind Maps also boost the associative thinking process, which is exactly what you need when organising your time and actions. You capture more, which allows you to manage your time better and makes you more effective.

Mind Maps, created by iMindMap software, showing how to organise information effectively

Creating Mind Map 'templates' to plan your actions

If a few minutes spent creating a Mind Map every morning can save you many more throughout the day, it follows that it's well worth spending a little while making up a template for your daily tasks.

If you regularly create a Mind Map for the same task, you could pre-draw the central image and main branches on a sheet of paper that you can photocopy, or you can use iMindMap software and print out the finished Mind Maps each morning.

Below are a couple of simple template suggestions, with the central image and branches pre-drawn; you can use these as a starting point and develop your own templates for whatever planning activities you do regularly. Remember, you can always add extra main branches if you need to when filling in the Mind Maps.

A computer-based Mind Map template (iMindMap software) for planning weekly tasks

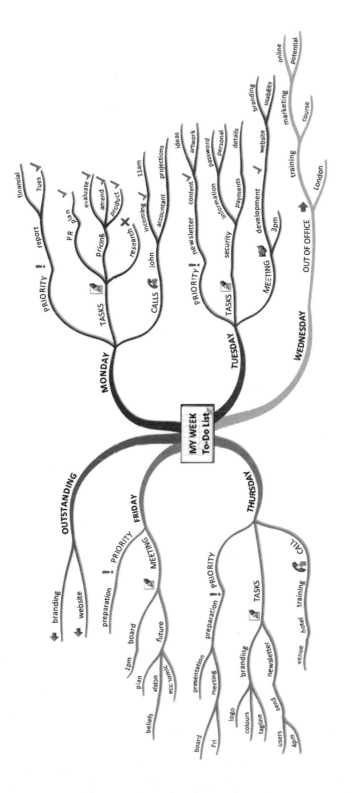

An example of a weekly to-do list created using iMindMap

Sharing the load

These organisational Mind Maps are invaluable tools for individuals to manage their workload, but they can also be used just as effectively for group or team-based Mind Mapping.

Both the manager and the team can benefit from this type of work planning, which also serves to improve communication within the business, so that everyone knows who is doing what, for when, and how. When everyone has this information easily to hand in a clear, logical Mind Map format, it allows individual team members and the manager to get on with their assigned tasks, happy in the knowledge that the other jobs are being taken care of. This is the ideal scenario for a business to work at maximum efficiency.

From the perspective of the team, these 'to-do' Mind Maps allow colleagues to take in the whole picture of their collective workload at a glance, while being able to focus in on the tasks ahead for the week and view the goals simply. This in turn enables everyone to plan their time in the way that suits them and which means that they can accomplish all their tasks.

A team Mind Map also shows colleagues the overall picture so that individuals can see and therefore understand the responsibilities and priorities of others, and also check if and when any of their own tasks are associated or connected to any of those of their colleagues. Team members should take responsibility for ticking off the tasks that they have completed, which is satisfying for them, allows others to know that the work has been done, and can help to motivate others to achieve their goals too.

The manager also benefits from this collaborative planning; using the team Mind Map they can create their own individual 'to-do' Mind Map for their week and workload. This allows them to plan their time quickly and easily – with no spreadsheets or complicated tables, fewer documents to manage and no need to link into different systems, while also being able to manage and review the team's tasks and time speedily (you can see in 30 seconds what would take 30 minutes to read in a linear note form), and divide tasks into sub-tasks to ensure the work is being divided fairly and efficiently and the jobs are assigned to the most appropriate people.

When using computer Mind Maps the manager's individual Mind Map can link any task to web sources, documents, spreadsheets and graphics, and connect tasks to other tasks or link different team members' tasks using relationship arrows. At a glance the manager can grasp an overview of the week ahead, and also print out the overview for personal easy reference or even project it onto a wall at a meeting at the beginning of the week using computer Mind Mapping. At the end of each week the manager's and the team's Mind Maps can be reviewed and even discussed all together to establish which goals have and have not been achieved and why that was the case, enabling everyone to offer suggestions as to how deadlines and workload could be tackled more successfully in future.

Monthly and annual Mind Map planning

If your business requires longer-term planning for projects and deadlines, you could also use a Mind Map to list tasks that need completing on a monthly or even annual basis.

The Mind Map below shows typical main branches that you could create for a monthly plan, on which you can mark appointments and meetings that you have scheduled, visualise personal and professional development, or even assign a branch for each project that you are working on.

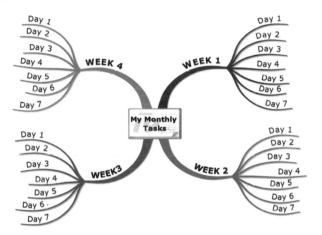

You can also use a Mind Map to plan your year very effectively too.

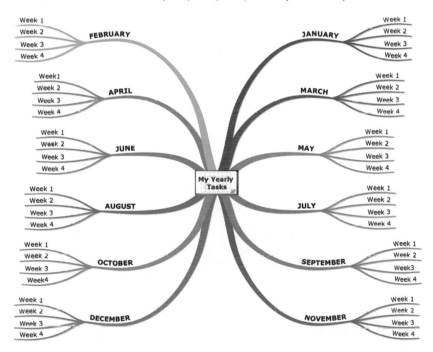

1 Start with the central image, such as 'marketing team', and add the main branches – perhaps divided up into team member's names. If you are going to institute this approach on a weekly basis, make a template 'team to-do' Mind Map to make the weekly work allocation process even quicker.

2 Draw your 'child' or sub-branches for each main branch (member of staff) and label these with the key task that you would like that person to achieve by the end of the week.

3 Schedule a team meeting for Monday mornings and email the completed Mind Map to each member of the team in good time for them to be able to print it off and look at it in advance. At the meeting, use the Mind Map to talk through everyone's tasks and objectives for the week.

4 On Friday afternoon, hold another team meeting or individual meeting (manager and team member) and again use the Mind Map to see what has been achieved and to discuss any issues or problems that arose in relation to carrying out the tasks.

Mind Mapping your telephone calls

There's nothing more frustrating than putting down the phone after a telephone call and struggling to remember sections of the conversation, or, worse still, missing key points because you're busy scribbling down what is being said. This is true of individual calls and also of conference calls, when vital information can be lost by simply not being able to keep up or remember facts.

So next time you make an important business or conference call, use a Mind Map to keep a record of the main points of the conversation.

A Mind Map for note-taking in a telephone call

The example opposite has the following four branches: the main points of what was said; the actions required by each person; the key ideas; and other general items of interest or concern that the call flagged up. Before or after the call, record the name of the person and the date on which the conversation took place in the corner of the page so that you can reference it easily later.

Mind Maps for note-taking

For many people, taking notes during a meeting, a planning session or a training course can be a real nightmare. Like emails, meetings are a necessary but incredibly time-consuming feature of the workplace. Minutes or notes always need to be taken to get the most out of any meeting, particularly when brainstorming or discussing objectives or agendas.

If the information to be noted is well structured the job is not too painful, but in reality information 'senders' tend to jump from one subject to another. When the information 'sender' gets carried away by their own associative thought processes, the question for the note-taker becomes, 'What should I write down?' and 'Where should I put that piece of information?', and the flow of ideas coming through is blocked. But with a Mind Map, if the speaker jumps from one subject to another the Mind Mapper can also freely jump from one 'branch' to another along with the speaker, so a Mind Mapper will come away with far more information to hand than their conventional note-taking colleague.

This is because Mind Maps by their nature are generative, which means they are designed to allow people to radiate new ideas in any direction, whereas linear note-taking is 'selective', i.e. we note down our best ideas (or at least what we think are our best ideas). The latter approach is risky, since by being selective in what we write we limit our ability to generate new thoughts or ideas which could be infinitely more powerful.

Standard note-taking is sequential: when we finish one sentence, we start the next. It is a 'blinkered' thought process. A Mind Map, on the other hand, opens up your thoughts in all directions, enabling you to create associations that would not have been possible using normal note-taking methods. You are not forced to put down what you think are your best ideas, you are free to put down any and all ideas.

This is just one advantage that Mind Maps have over standard note-taking. Mind Mapping also means that the more important ideas are immediately recognisable at the centre and the relative importance of each offshoot idea is visually pinpointed, so you can see at a glance what's important and what isn't. The links between key concepts are also immediately identifiable via keywords, which encourages the association of ideas and concepts and improving memory.

Mind Maps come into their own after the meeting, too. Their clear structure means that you can rapidly review any information collated in the meeting, add to any branches of thought easily and even revisit the Mind Map to make the information contained within it more memorable for easier recall later.

It is useful to know who said what at a meeting, and Mind Maps are an excellent and simple way of placing all team members' contributions in context. Including *all* individual contributions on the Mind Map will increase the energy, enthusiasm and cooperation within the group as they will see that their ideas and input are noted and valued.

By creating a Mind Map of a meeting, each member of the group has a complete record of the discussions, thus ensuring that everyone understands and remembers exactly what has been proposed or agreed. The mnemonic nature of Mind Maps greatly increases the likelihood that everyone's memory of the meeting will be virtually perfect, and the visual nature and one word per branch makes them far more condensed and viewable on a single page than normal meeting summaries that range from 5 to 30 pages!

The compact nature of a Mind Map meeting summary means that the discussions that took place can easily be reviewed at a later date, even when long periods of time have passed.

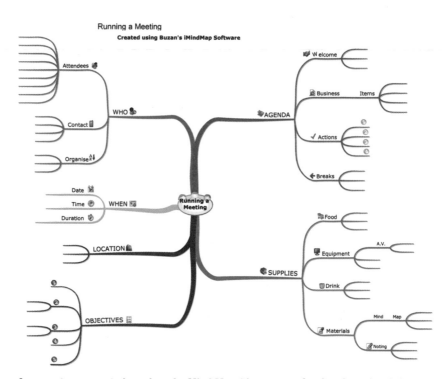

A computer-generated version of a Mind Map (the process for drawing a hand-drawn version can be seen on pages 30–2)

Mind Mapping for core business skills

Simple steps to note-taking with a Mind Map

If you have a clear idea of the agenda of the meeting you will be attending beforehand, you can use this information to create a structure for your Mind Map before you start taking notes.

Add the main topics you expect to be covered to the main branches of your Mind Map. You can also add onto your Mind Map any questions you may have. If there is no clear structure given beforehand, add some empty main branches to your central image; they will allow you to jump very quickly from one part of your Mind Map to another.

In the same way, you can also use templates to facilitate your note-taking. Add the keywords of your template onto the main branches of your Mind Map. For example, the 6Ws of sustainable corporate growth (who, what, where, why, when, how), or SWOT (strengths, weaknesses, opportunities, threats) or PNI (positive, negative, interesting).

Note down the incoming information using words and pictures and jump from one branch to another, if necessary. If you are a Mind Map beginner you will sometimes notice that you write down far too much in phrases and sentences. Do not worry about this; you will quickly make progress and note down less and less because you will come to realise that with only a few keywords your amazing brain will be able to retrieve all the information. Once you've mastered the technique, you will find you have more time to participate and engage 'intelligently' in meetings and discussions.

The flow of information in meetings is sometimes so fast that you will not have enough time even to change coloured pens. Again, do not worry about this. Use a single colour if you have to; however, if you want to remember the information from your Mind Map, adding colours and drawings will help your brain considerably. If you can, redraw or colour-highlight your Mind Map in the 24 hours after the session so that the information is memorable.

If you realise that you have missed something, draw an empty main or second-level branch where you think you 'lost' it. At the end of the communication, these empty branches will 'blink', reminding you to ask questions to get the information you need to fill them in.

Finally, it also sometimes happens that you reach the border of the page while the information flow on that particular branch in your Mind Map keeps going. In that case, simply add a new page to your Mind Map and stick it to the starting page later on.

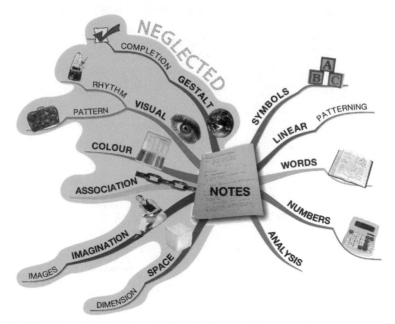

A Mind Map for note-taking in a meeting highlighting the natural functions that are neglected too often

Most meetings also involve presentations, and using Mind Maps to enhance your skill in presenting business ideas and new business development is explored in detail in Chapter 6.

Checklist for Mind Mapping a meeting

We have shown you how to Mind Map a meeting in Chapter 2, but in addition to the basic creative process remember:

- The subject of the meeting provides the central image.

- The major items on the agenda correspond to the main branches.

- As the meeting progresses you can add ideas and information wherever they seem most relevant.

- An alternative and effective method is to get each speaker to prepare a mini Mind Map and then cross-refer the themes and trends as they begin to emerge at the meeting.

- There is no need to worry if your Mind Map notes look 'messy'. They are simply reflecting the confused state of communication at that particular time, and can always be clarified and redirected later on.

- As well as individual Mind Maps you could have a master Mind Map on a large interactive whiteboard, projector screen or flipchart that is visible to all. In this way the facilitator can register every contribution and place it within the overall structure of the meeting.

How Mind Maps cut time and increased corporate clarity

Cliff Shaffran, founder and CEO of Q3global, utilises Mind Maps to review his monthly boardroom meetings and outcomes. Q3global was formed in the 1980s, when Cliff used to run monthly board meetings recorded in standard minutes. At the end of the year the twelve sets of minutes were distributed to the board members for their annual three-day review of the year and planning for the next.

The three days of review and planning were almost totally packed with reviewing these minutes. In 1993, when Cliff discovered Mind Maps, he provided each of the company directors with the agenda of the meeting in Mind Map form. As the meeting progressed, each director mind mapped the development of the meeting. At the end of the meeting each director checked with the Mind Maps the others had prepared and they all agreed on them – so the Mind Maps became the minutes of the meeting.

A prime Mind Map was created which contained everyone's individual thoughts. Traditionally at the end of the year Cliff's company had a directors' three-day year-end review and new planning session. Families came along too as part of the outing while the directors reviewed all the minutes and planning for the future. They had twelve meetings (one for each month), which they mind mapped and then ended each one with a large Mind Map. These collective Mind Maps were colour-coded for actions, tasks completed, priorities, projects, challenges, and so on. Any director looking at them could instantly see their own position within the Mind Map or the functions that related to them and the company's ongoing progression. On a large table they placed the twelve monthly Mind Map summaries in order from January to December and simply by walking up and down could instantly see everything about the company. It was a highly motivating scenario, with 'tasks accomplished' ticked off and a superb overview snapshot provided.

As a result, planning the next year was almost accomplished for them by the annual review Mind Maps and the new-year planning Mind Map was effectively laid out for them. What had taken three days was achieved in half a day. What did they do with the other two-and-a-half days? The directors decided extremely brain-consciously that they would stay together for those days – touring, dining and relaxing. They found that in those two-and-a-half days of 'blue sky' freedom they generated far more creative and innovative ideas for the following year and years than they had ever done in those linear, prison-like annual reviews in the past. Cliff concludes:

> Maps have been a core component of the 'thinking structure', not only of our Board, but our company's operations ever since. In fact, 80 per cent of our corporate documentation and internal messaging is now on Mind Maps. We achieve far greater clarity in all our communication, develop more creative ideas faster and save volumes of time daily using Mind Maps. In essence – we get more done.

Mismanaging emails

Poor handling of email isn't just a problem of time management, it's a communications fiasco that seriously fractures businesses thinking. It also reinforces our reliance on linear thinking as we scroll our emails and word processors up and down like a lift.

This stifles creativity. Why? Because with linear thinking your brain always 'hooks up' from where it left off – the last full stop, the last line. This is even more true when using a computer and word processing software. Email etiquette is a brain destroyer; there is no freedom of thought, no freedom of association, and nowhere for your mind to wander, meander and look at the big picture.

Mind Maps for email efficiency

You can use Mind Maps to significantly upgrade the efficiency of your email correspondence in a number of ways.

- Run through your incoming emails before replying to them, and for each draw a branch and note any connections and what you have to do or whom you have to call. Draw up a paper Mind Map 'response chart' before you do any actual keying in when replying to an email.

- Assign specific time periods in the day to the writing of emails. More random approaches oblige you to multi-task to an unacceptable degree and force your brain to change its focus. Consequently you waste your time, energy and brain cells.

- If you draw up a Mind Map plan of your day you can add a separate Mind Map branch for emails you intend to compose or send out that day. In this way you'll be able to cluster emails by similar subjects or by receiver and therefore give your brain far greater focus to stay 'in the groove'. At the same time you can derive satisfaction and a sense of accomplishment as you tick off those messages you have successfully sent.

- Many emails are short responses and will not require a Mind Map; for emails that cover important subjects and so will require a large number of words, use a quick Mind Map to organise your thoughts and prioritise what's important.

By using a Mind Map to organise your emails in this way, the very few minutes you spend composing them will save you many more minutes and even hours of your time later.

Example

Here is a graphic example from South Korea showing how Mind Maps and emails make for efficient data sharing. This approach is used by Park Sang Hoon, who has been engaged in Korea's online advertising market since 1999 and is recognised for his know-how and marketing abilities in that field. He cites Mind Maps for leading him to success. He is a marketing team leader in OPMS for an online advertising agency.

One of Park Sang Hoon's major duties is to support his business colleagues. Whenever he obtains material that will be helpful to advertisers, he posts the materials on the blog, which is operated as a public-relations exercise by the company.

When the materials are posted on the blog, they are presented as well-organised Mind Maps so the whole contents can be seen 'to view'.

After posting the materials, Mr Park then emails his business colleagues to alert them that there are materials on the blog. When he sends the message by email, he includes a Mind Map summary, again so all the materials are viewable in one 'hit'.

The above process has several advantages:

- You don't need to download any materials because the Mind Map summary provides the whole content of the materials.

- You can save yourself time because you can judge at first sight which material is worthy of downloading.

- Blog posting using Mind Maps gives vigour and diversity to an otherwise text-centred blog, which is apt to be hard and dry.

- Disseminating information by using Mind Maps makes it possible for the reader to process that information much more effectively.

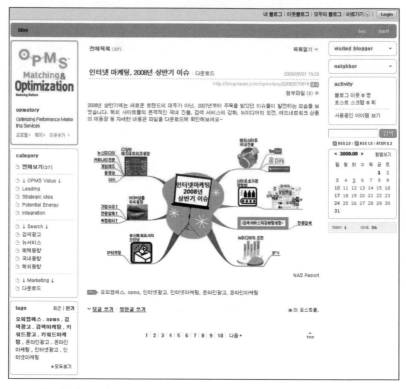

An example of a South Korean Mind Map posted onto a blog

Getting your thoughts, arguments and ideas in place ready for discussions with clients or colleagues is a key part of getting organised and an important factor in achieving the results you want in business. In many situations, success in business comes down to negotiating and securing a deal. Here again preparation is key, and the next chapter will demonstrate how fundamental Mind Maps can be in the process of negotiation and getting the outcome you want or need.

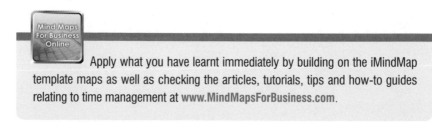

Apply what you have learnt immediately by building on the iMindMap template maps as well as checking the articles, tutorials, tips and how-to guides relating to time management at www.MindMapsForBusiness.com.

Mind Mapping for negotiations

One of the things that comes to mind that I think is highly relevant to Mind Mapping is that the skilled negotiator thinks in terms of options, the less-skilled negotiator thinks in terms of limitations. One of the kisses of death in negotiation is to be predictable – if you can use Mind Mapping you can think in terms of multiple paths and that is one of the things I train people in all the time.

PROFESSOR KATHLEEN KELLY, management consultant

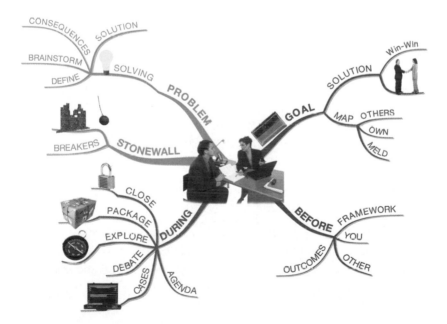

Mind Map summary for Chapter 5

The goal of any negotiation is to end up with some sort of agreement between all the parties involved so that everyone feels satisfied with the outcome; in other words, achieving a 'win–win solution'. True negotiation takes place when every party respects the others and their points of view, and enters into the discussion positively and openly. An important factor of successful negotiation is to go into the discussion armed with the information you need to convince others that your ideas are sound or preferable to another's. Laying them all down in a Mind Map before, during and after the negotiation meeting is an excellent way of facilitating this.

Each of us carries millions of Mind Maps in one giant 'internet of the brain', and each of our experiences of 'reality' is going to be different from the next person's. So the expression that 'the map is not the territory' (often heard around self-improvement techniques), can be explained as: 'the territory of the map in one brain is different from that in another brain'. Understanding this concept is crucial for communication and negotiation, and thus Mind Maps become a highly transparent and honest tool to facilitate 'map reading' of both 'territories'.

Negotiating – 'melding' Mind Maps

The first goal of negotiation is to explore and understand the Mind Map of the person with whom you are negotiating. Secondly, you need to make sure you communicate your Mind Map – the map of your territory – to the person with whom you are negotiating. Thirdly, you need to merge or 'meld' the Mind Maps of each party.

Successful negotiation will allow both sides to reach an agreement that enables them to create a new Mind Map, a new territory, which is a neutral. In order to achieve this goal you need to jot down your facts, statistics, ideas – whatever information you need to structure a convincing argument – onto a Mind Map. Laying out your thoughts in this way helps you to visualise a win–win strategy and then go on to implement it, using the Mind Map as reference during your negotiation.

If, for example, you are having trouble negotiating the price of a product with a potential customer, using a Mind Map to explore other avenues for debate or compromise will enable you to come up with a new gambit to allow you to continue negotiation. Without a Mind Map you might have given up or given in.

However, Mind Map or no Mind Map, it is important to know when to compromise. If you are reaching an impasse in negotiations because you are determined that your solution and only your solution is the correct one, that is not negotiation – that is dictatorship. That kind of attitude will lead only to resentment, which will stifle business creativity and productivity.

How to mind map your way to an ideal settlement

So, with a little thought before your meeting a Mind Map can help you chart your way through each stage of a negotiation successfully, thereby increasing the chance that the outcome will be positive for both parties.

Creating a Mind Map before entering into a negotiation will ensure that you arrive at the meeting well prepared, which will give you a strong advantage from the off. During the negotiation you can use Mind Maps to help you manage the whole process with confidence; from laying down your goals and those of the other side, to exploring alternatives and bargaining for the final agreement. If you encounter deadlocks or reach an impasse along the way you can use your Mind Maps to find a way through the issues and overcome difficulties in negotiations.

So let's examine in detail how you can use Mind Maps in each of these stages to get the result you want.

Before negotiating

Before you negotiate it is a good idea to prepare thoroughly so that you enter the negotiation situation with superior knowledge and understanding of both your position and that of the other party. A Mind Map is the perfect framework for your research; it helps you break down the fundamental aspects and variables of the negotiation in a way that still enables you to see the bigger picture. Entering a meeting armed with your Mind Map will also increase your confidence on the day as you will feel prepared and will be ready for any sudden turns in the negotiation process.

First, create a central image to represent what it is you are negotiating over and give it a title, if you like. Following the principles of Mind Mapping, add the main themes that you can investigate as part of your preparation on strong branches radiating out from the central image, then expand these ideas into sub-branches as you work. To ensure your Mind Map preparation covers all angles, try using the following topic structure for your main and sub branches:

● **You** – Your goals, personal motives, needs, wants and boundaries.

● **The other party** – Their goals, values and beliefs, emotional tendencies, needs, wants and expectations.

● **Potential outcomes** – The consequences of winning or losing, alternatives, trades, power and possible solutions.

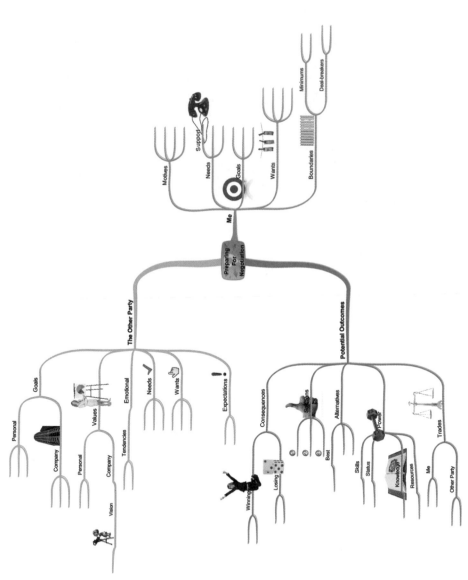

Preparing For Negotiation

Me
- Motives
- Support
- Needs
- Goals
- Wants
- Boundaries
  - Minimums
  - Deal-breakers

The Other Party
- Goals
  - Personal
  - Company
- Values
  - Personal
  - Company
  - Vision
- Emotional
  - Tendencies
- Needs
- Wants
- Expectations

Potential Outcomes
- Consequences
  - Winning
  - Losing
- Solutions
  - Best
- Alternatives
- Power
  - Skills
  - Status
  - Knowledge
  - Resources
- Trades
  - Me
  - Other Party

A Mind Map for preparing for negotiations

You

Consider the following pointers when you are evaluating yourself, and let your thoughts and ideas flow naturally to determine what you truly want to gain from the negotiation. Try to integrate lots of images to stimulate your thinking and show emphasis and connections through colour, highlights, numbers, symbols, codes and links.

1 Your goals

First off, it is absolutely key to any negotiation that you outline the goals and outcomes you would like to achieve, e.g. more time, more money, more benefits, and so on. Be as specific as possible. Knowing exactly what you would like to obtain from the negotiation will give you more negotiating power. You can also weight your goals in order of priority using numbers or symbols to help you keep your focus on what is most important.

2 Your personal motives

Determine what is driving you towards the goals and objectives you have laid out for yourself. Are your motives aligned with your highest ideals, values and standards? If not, realign them so that they sum up what is most important for you on the biggest scale. Link your motives to their relevant goals using relationship arrows.

3 Your needs

Identify clearly and concisely the needs that you would like to satisfy as a result of this negotiation. These are effectively the unconditional and non-negotiable requirements that are absolutely necessary to you or your business. These are not to be confused with your wants (see below), which are essentially the things that ideally it would be great to have but wouldn't cause damage or debilitation to your business if you didn't obtain agreement on them.

Mind Mapping your needs will help you to see what is most valuable to you or your business so you are better able to position yourself during the negotiation process and ensure that you do achieve these, even if you end up compromising on your wants. For example, retaining a reliable client or your company's reputation may be a need for your negotiation situation, whereas agreeing a specific price would just be a want.

4 Your wants

Here you can consider the list of demands that you would also like to have as part of the negotiation. These will be more of a wish list, and some of these might end up being the 'sacrifice' points that you can add in to your starting position to give yourself room to manoeuvre during the negotiation.

5 Your boundaries

It is important to be clear about your boundaries so that you are aware of what concessions you can afford to give to a settlement. Consider the minimum terms that you will accept for each of your goals and identify your deal-breaker points, i.e. the points at which you will end the negotiation. For example, a salesperson may set himself a non-negotiable limit on giving a discount on price beyond 10 per cent.

The other party

Once you have assessed yourself, you can then embark on a thorough investigation of the other party. Consider their business from a variety of angles and perspectives so that you have enough information to help you respond optimally to what you predict might be their actions and standpoints during the negotiation. You won't be able to foresee everything that they will bring up in the discussion, but creating a clear and detailed Mind Map before the meeting might give you confidence and help you to find answers to their arguments without being taken off guard.

1 The other party's goals

The other party will most likely come to the table with two objectives: the goals they would like to achieve on a personal level, and those they desire on a company level. In order to achieve a successful outcome for yourself you need to anticipate what these goals are likely to be.

- **Personal goals** – It is a good idea to weigh up how important you think each of their personal objectives, goals and outcomes will be, so that you are aware of which ones will most affect their decision-making ability. Use numbers or symbols to rank them in order of importance. Connect any goals that you both share using relationship arrows, as these links can be utilised to build rapport during the negotiation.

- **Company goals** – If the other party is representing a company or organisation you will need to identify their overall goals and objectives. Knowing this will enable you to get a picture of their long-term outlook, and you can use this knowledge to structure your argument to demonstrate to them how your set of goals fits in with theirs.

2 The other party's values and beliefs

Just as the other party will have two different standpoints for their objectives, they will also come to a negotiation bringing with them two different sets of values. Most employees will know and work with their company's values, but every individual will hold another set of personal values which may differ in some respects. Your job is to identify these and mind map the way in which these might work together or against each other in negotiations.

- **Personal values** – Try to clarify how the other party views the world and how they prioritise their life, decisions and actions. Their belief and value patterns can strongly influence their decision-making ability and reveal hidden fears that you can capitalise on during the negotiation process.

- **Company values (vision and mission)** – Reviewing a company's vision and mission statement helps give you an insight into the values, beliefs and principles that a company seeks to project through their reputation. It also reveals whether a company is conservative and risk-averse or more likely to take chances. You can harness this knowledge to align your arguments with the main principles of the negotiating party.

3 The other party's emotional tendencies

You can build emotions into the Mind Map by placing a branch that highlights perhaps a tendency of being too emotionally driven by a product and being too defensive about it (and so believing it is worth much more). Recognising this in your Mind Map enables you to weigh up emotionally charged issues (which are hard to jettison in negotiations) pragmatically, and see how they are impacting your thinking. This leads to a much clearer and analytical 'map of the territory'.

4 The other party's needs

Understanding your counterpart's distinct needs can help you develop a constructive negotiation approach so you can obtain the things that are important to you, yet still satisfy their basic needs. For example, as a property agent negotiating the price of a house with an interested couple, you would need to determine what is most important to them. Is it location, size and space, or price? Understanding what they need to achieve from the sale of their house can help you determine what they will settle for when the negotiation is finalised, and therefore how you can bring about a rewarding agreement for all concerned.

5 The other party's wants

Discovering what the other side wants from you during the negotiation is crucial if you are going to be able to illustrate that their wants are clearly not in your best interest. Understanding their wants in advance of the negotiation can also help you to decide in advance what you are willing to concede – if that discussion should arise. Mind Mapping these options will give you more leeway to develop a mutually beneficial agreement just by glancing at your Mind Map during the negotiation, rather than having to think on your feet. You can subdivide this topic with branches that focus on the aspects they may want, such as a 'specific action', 'material possessions', 'an agreement to do something' and even your 'knowledge or experience', and subdivide it further with other wants that you might be willing to compromise on.

6 The other party's expectations

Finally, you must use your research to collate an understanding of your counterpart's overall expectations when coming to the negotiation session. These expectations will effectively determine their strategy, approach and willingness to make concessions.

Evaluate potential outcomes and variables

After a thorough examination of the other party your next step is to take some time to assess the potential outcomes and variables of the negotiation. Variables are options that will help you find agreement with the other party. Here are some points you can consider for your sub-branches:

Consequences (of winning or losing)

What are the consequences for you of winning or losing this negotiation? What are the consequences for the other party? Having this understanding can prepare you to make more effective decisions and to be aware of possible opportunities or obstacles that may arise during the negotiation.

Alternatives

If you don't reach an agreement initially with the other party, what alternatives could you propose? What alternatives might the other party have in mind? How will these affect you – are they potentially good or bad for your interests? If forced to choose, which might be your best alternative?

Before the negotiations begin, create a Mind Map to predict what some of these alternatives might be. Take the central issue and allow your thoughts to branch off to offer other solutions. Write them all down for now – you may think you will not use some of them in negotiation, but you might find that when all other compromises are rejected these will offer a good starting point for another discussion. Having alternatives is an important element of negotiation, as being able to climb down from hard stances and meet the other party halfway can make a crucial difference to the outcome of the negotiation.

Trades

Your trades are the negotiating factors that you are potentially prepared to give away to reach a favourable outcome. Essentially you must determine what it is that the other party perceives as valuable that you could trade in order to entice them into agreement. Also, what could the other party potentially trade in order to motivate you to agree to their terms? What do you each feel comfortable giving away?

In order to predict where these concessions can be made you need to determine who holds the influential power within the negotiation. Use sub-branches to mind map who you think has control over critical 'resources', 'knowledge', 'status' and 'skills'.

Also, consider who stands to lose the most if agreement isn't reached. An understanding of the power balance in the relationship helps you better prepare the ways in which you might be able to weaken the other party's position and strengthen your own within the negotiation.

Once you've mind mapped all these considerations, see what possible compromises there might be. Complete your Mind Map marking in these potential solutions.

What if you don't have enough time to prepare in detail?

If a negotiation meeting is called at short notice and you don't have much time to prepare for it, or are overwhelmed with the thought of mind mapping out all the variables of the negotiation process, a good starting point is just to mind map the potential areas of agreement and disagreement that you think could feature.

The joy of Mind Maps is that they can be as detailed or basic as you wish them to be and they don't take long to create – particularly if they are for your own use and therefore not required to be immaculately drawn for a presentation. Even through the simplest of Mind Maps you can gain a solid understanding of the other party's approach to the discussion and determine what potential obstacles might need mitigating and which opportunities you could capitalise on during the negotiation.

During negotiations

So the time has come to get round the table and start negotiating. You've prepared well and now you can use your Mind Map simply to state your case to the other party, ensuring that you get all your main points across and retain your focus. However, the role of your Mind Map doesn't need to end here; with participation from the other party you can create a Mind Map template in advance of the meeting and then use it throughout the discussion to structure and record the contributions to the negotiation of both parties.

Using a Mind Map during negotiations

You can fill in a Mind Map to record negotiations along much the same lines as you would minute a meeting (see page 68), then at the end of the discussions you can use this new Mind Map as a tool to help all the participants reach a conclusion that satisfies both parties.

You don't have to follow a strictly sequential path when creating a Mind Map during negotiations; both parties can easily jump between the different sections to add sub-branches as and when thoughts occur. As there are no constraints to the process, both parties' creativity can flourish and so it can be much more comfortable to work together to find viable options.

Once you have created a central image and title for the negotiation the steps listed below can be used as headings for your main branches, helping you build a logical and balanced overview of the negotiation. The Mind Map can include as much detail as you wish, simply by adding more sub-branches.

Use these steps as guidelines for how to create a Mind Map that will reflect the arguments put forward during your negotiation, but as with any Mind Map, feel free to add your own personal touches that relate to your particular circumstances.

1 Agenda

Establish what are the main elements being negotiated, particularly the key issues that need to be discussed. Suggested sub-branches include:

- **Subject** – what needs to be discussed and agreed?
- **People** – who will be involved and what will be their roles in the negotiation?
- **Timescales** – what timescales are both parties working towards?
- **Issues** – what are the major issues that need to be agreed, e.g. price, delivery schedule, payment terms, packaging, quality of product, length of contract?

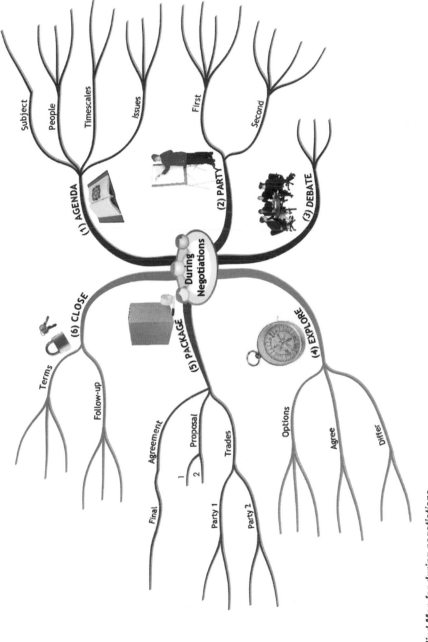

Subject

People

Timescales

Issues

First

Second

(1) AGENDA

(2) PARTY

(3) DEBATE

During Negotiations

(6) CLOSE

(5) PACKAGE

(4) EXPLORE

Terms

Follow-up

Agreement

Proposal

1

2

Trades

Final

Party 1

Party 2

Options

Agree

Differ

A Mind Map for during negotiations

At this stage, issues should be kept general and no concessions should be made or agreements reached until both parties' cases have been presented.

2 Party

Obviously your Mind Map should allow for the cases of each party to be included, whether the negotiation is between individuals or companies.

Create branches while you state your case to the other party. This will mainly consist of a shopping list of what you would like from the negotiation, backed up by the logical and emotional insights you gained during your preparation. Then state your ultimate goal clearly so that the other party understands exactly what it is you need. When stating your case, aim as high as you can justify in order to gain the best deal for yourself. Bear in mind that the other party will try to bring down your position later in the negotiation and it is much easier to be brought down from objectives than to gain them.

When it is the other party's turn to mind map their arguments you can help to clarify their position by listening properly to what they are saying and gently probing for understanding through questions that will help you determine their legitimate wants. By listening in a total way you will be able to understand more clearly where they stand in relation to the points that you have drawn up on your part of the Mind Map.

3 Debate

This phase gives each party a chance to strengthen their case further through two-way discussion, and strategically this is the best time to try to expose weaknesses in the other party's position.

The 'debate' branch of the Mind Map should be used to record any additional arguments that may arise. The collaborative nature of creating a Mind Map in this way means that there is little possibility for misinterpretation afterwards.

When debating it is a good idea to use your research to make logical arguments and to provide strong evidence in support of the claims you are making. Also, use your understanding of the emotional tendencies and values of the other party to persuade them to your way of thinking.

4 Explore

After thorough debate you will be ready to explore possible options and variables that you have not previously discussed. For example, if you are negotiating payment terms you could consider options for allowing extra time for payment, or payment in instalments or in relation to performance. Include these options on the Mind Map.

Exploring options is an important part of the negotiation process as it helps you to uncover the areas of agreement and difference that you presented earlier on. Highlight these areas on your Mind Map and connect any links between various elements of the negotiation. At this stage the Mind Map comes into its own, as it is an extremely useful visual tool that will allow you to gauge clearly where your path and that of the other side lie, at a glance.

5 Package

The effective packaging of proposals for areas of compromise will assist you to gain greater leverage at this stage of the negotiation process. Check your Mind Map sporadically throughout the negotiation discussions to see if you can identify any areas in which trade-offs could be suggested on both sides if it looks as if an agreement is not going to be reached and a compromise might be required. If the discussions so far have not highlighted any such areas, you could offer conditional proposals in the meeting about specific aspects of the negotiation and add these to the Mind Map. Rank or weight each proposal to aid the final analysis and agreement.

The crucial point about any compromise is not to give anything away without getting something in return. For example, a salesperson could offer ten hours of additional training in return for a client agreeing to be a reference for their next six prospects. Typically this process of bargaining will lead to an agreement being reached. However, be wary about making concessions on issues for which you are not prepared.

6 Close

Close the deal by agreeing to the terms of the arrangement; making sure you have established a favourable outcome for yourself and all parties concerned. Chart on the Mind Map the terms of agreement and how the arrangement will be followed up.

Using mind-mapping software during your negotiation really speeds up the finalisation of the agreement; there no longer needs to be a delay while confirmation of the deal is written up. Mind Maps can be quickly printed so both parties walk away with a fully signed-off record of the negotiation. What's more, Mind Maps can be exported into a variety of formats, such as PDF or image files, to make it much easier to distribute the conclusions of the meeting to colleagues.

Troubleshooting negotiations

You were fully prepared and conducted yourself well during the negotiation, yet you still find yourself at a deadlock or impasse with the other party. Perhaps there is an issue or condition that neither of you seem to be able to agree on and this is obstructing the chance of a settlement?

Surprisingly, many breakdowns during negotiation are the result of simple human factors like personality differences, fear of losing face, or merely an inability to make a decision.

The best way to overcome such obstacles is to use the Mind Map with your negotiation partner to come up with win–win opportunities. Mind Mapping removes the face-to-face conflict and allows both parties to work together to create a favourable outcome. By giving you both control over all relevant information within a secure and systematic framework, Mind Mapping encourages you to focus on the 'big picture'; to see beyond the challenges.

In order to reach a mutually advantageous solution, you can use a Mind Map to identify 'stonewall breakers' so that you can find a way through, or simply for creative problem-solving. Both approaches are ideal for averting conflict and breaking down negotiating obstacles, so it is up to you to employ whichever method you feel will be most useful for your specific negotiation challenge.

Use a Mind Map to identify 'stonewall breakers'

Mind Maps give you options, they give you the edge, so instead of focusing on one or two things you get myriad ways of getting over the wall, under the wall and around that wall, rather than crashing against it.

If you work with the other party you will be able to create a Mind Map that enables you to evaluate a range of factors that could help you break down the obstacles to negotiation. These factors can be considered in the light of the entire negotiation or merely in relation to a specific issue or condition that is causing problems. Mind Mapping these factors creates an open climate in which new alternatives can be developed, and encourages both parties to be more receptive to alternatives.

Colour-coding and numbers or symbols can be used to rank your best or worst options as an instant visual aid to show you whether you are reaching a measured and satisfying conclusion. Some 'stonewall breakers' that you could consider for your main branches include:

- **Money** – If you are at a deadlock over an issue regarding payments, consider alternative approaches as to how you can structure or form the way in which money is paid, rather than the amount. For example, agree that a larger deposit should be made, or negotiate a shorter payment period or different payment scheme.

- **People** – If the deadlock is down to clashes of personality around the negotiating table, see if you can change the people who are involved in implementing the negotiation agreement. Try allocating a new team leader or team members.

- **Risk** – Change the scope of risk-sharing between you; for example, consider sharing losses or gains that could result from the negotiation, in order to restore trust between the two sides.

- **Timescales** – Adjust the timescale allocated for performance. For example, agree for project milestones to be deferred in the initial months to allow more time to get going on a project, yet keep later targets the same so that the overall deadline is still met.

- **Reschedule** – To eliminate some uncertainty, consider postponing some difficult parts of the agreement to a later date when you have had the chance to conduct more research.

- **Protection** – Instil greater security and ensure satisfaction by recommending grievance procedures and guarantees.

- **Contract** – Change the type of contract that you could use. Types you could consider include a fixed price or scaled price contract, contracts based on time or contracts based on percentages, e.g. percentage of savings, percentage of increased sales or percentage of profit created.

- **Terms** – Think about changes in the specifications or terms of the agreement.

Based on all relevant considerations, complete your Mind Map by including the solutions that you have reached (see example overleaf).

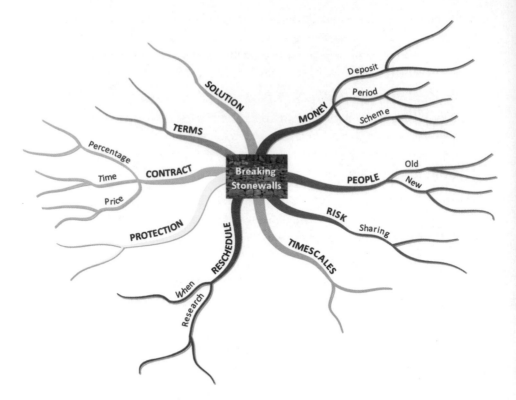

A Mind Map showing 'stonewall breakers'

Use a Mind Map for creative problem-solving

When confronted with a deadlock situation during the negotiation, all too often both parties wrestle with the problem and try to 'force' a solution. Straining in this way will rarely result in a favourable solution and will only serve to increase stress. Mind Mapping is a far more effective way to attain clarity and find a way around the problem in a more harmonious fashion.

By using the problem that you have come across as the central image you can work together to radiate thoughts, ideas and possible solutions. The following pointers can help you structure your branches:

● **Define** – Ask a set of open-ended questions that will help you define the problem clearly. Focus on the what, when, where, why, who and how of the problem. For instance, where did this problem first appear? How is this problem influencing other areas? Answering these questions will open up new understandings that are critical to the effectiveness of later stages in the problem-solving process.

- **Brainstorm** – Use free association to envisage lots of ideas for possible solutions and strategies. Do not take the time to evaluate the ideas at this stage; the more flexibility of thought you allow now, the more effective your problem-solving will be later on.

- **Consequences** – Anticipate the likely consequences of putting your different solutions into practice. Consider both the benefits and drawbacks of each solution to help you decide which one to act upon.

- **Solution** – Agree which solution would best help you solve your negotiation problem. Break it down into a set of logical 'to-do' steps.

If you follow the steps for negotiating with a Mind Map as outlined above, you will be able to look forward and anticipate such scenarios positively, knowing that there is always a solution, rather than go into negotiations as tense, combative, frustrating, antagonistic, draining and often unsuccessful experiences. The mere fact that the two sides have come together to negotiate must indicate that you think you can achieve a mutually realisable conclusion that will allow you to join forces, and the combined Mind Map or 'Mind Map meld' allows you to do that.

Seijo Naito's story: Negotiating the family business

This story, about a highly regarded business in Japan – a prime provider of traditional ceremonial and house footwear – highlights how Mind Mapping helped steer negotiation and communication for a son to take over his father's business.

He wanted to pass on his knowledge and skills, but he couldn't pass them on. I wanted to understand them, but I couldn't find a good way to understand them.

SEIJO NAITO

I grew up above a shop where my mother and father worked hard from morning until late. My father was a craftsman who manufactured and sold a traditional line of Japanese footwear in the Gion district of Kyoto. Here there was handiwork, established routines, traditions and many rules. Although it was small, the shop was loved by many people.

Eventually the time came when I, as an adult craftsman, was due to inherit the shop. However, it was very difficult to learn from my father what I needed to know to run the business. He had the temperament of a seasoned artisan and his own view of the world, passed down from generation to generation. I felt a sense of worthlessness and lack of ability, which he regarded with a sense of despair and great isolation. He feared the future because he felt that what he had inherited in his own generation could end up being lost. He wanted to pass on his knowledge and skills, but he couldn't pass them on. I wanted to understand them, but I couldn't find a good way to understand them. He tried hard to convey these things to me, but I couldn't understand them at all.

Untangling the threads

I had various roles in the business: as apprentice, subordinate, and son. These many kinds of standpoints also made the problem more complicated. We also felt very isolated from each other. I did not actually start using Mind Maps with very high expectations. However, they enabled me to unravel many tangled threads at a wonderful speed. It happened on a certain day: as usual, I went to my father's work and private room to discuss work-related matters. The discussion was about 'how the company should ideally be run and what the employees should be required to do from here on'.

I intended to talk to him with the aim of solving problems. However, at some point we started to attack each other's bad points, eventually ending up without reaching an agreement. Later that day I went back to talk to him, this time using a Mind Map. I politely said, 'Could you please talk to me?', but again what my father said was too abstract for me, and he did not answer my questions. Usually, I would start to get irritated at this point, but as I began to draw my Mind Map, I was able to concentrate on what I heard very naturally. When one hour had passed, I strangely said, 'It doesn't matter if I don't understand today', and I was able to feel very relaxed. When two hours had passed, I began to see the connections in front of my own eyes. I could now see that the conversation, which I thought had no relation at all with what I was talking about two hours earlier, was actually connected in the Mind Map.

Feeling surprised, I asked my father the following question, 'What you are saying now, does it mean this?' His answer surprised me even more. 'Didn't you know such things either? Haven't I explained them to you a thousand times?', he said. In fact, my father had always kindly explained things to me, but as I had not been able to discover the connections, what he said didn't make sense to me all. From then on, I understood the conversations more and more, as if I had reached the final chapter of a mystery novel or as if I had managed to solve a puzzle.

Our conversations that had been difficult to understand were now very enjoyable, and I always listened to what he said and wrote down the items in Mind Maps, which I then presented to my father. I heard subsequently through an acquaintance of my father's that he exclaimed, 'At last, he has understood as well', while looking at the Mind Maps I had sent to him. As the days have passed, using Mind Maps has become increasingly effective, and I have developed my ability to listen and my ability to express myself. Using Mind Maps has brought home to me what kind of outlook on the world my father had, what meanings his words had, and how far ahead into the future his words foresaw. In other words, it was clear to me that I had mistakenly thought we were seeing the same thing.

The use of Mind Maps also enabled me to sort out and understand things that were not in order and that were confused. As I became able to do this, I ended up understanding why my father insisted on passing on things by word of mouth and disliked putting things together in writing. This was because the world that I had been trying to understand from the start was too small for my father: he thought that the world that he could see himself was, of course, normal.

Some questions remain for me, though. Was our problem in communication and negotiation caused by our unusual occupation and this region, which entailed Kyoto's traditions, many rules and diverse kinds of knowledge? Or is this a common problem one might find in any workplace, family, or cherished community?

At first I thought it was only our special problem, but recently I have come to think that such problems probably occur in all places where there are people and things that we feel love and passion for and care about. I have come to recognise that handing down tradition orally to the next generation is negotiation, and that negotiation is not about winning or losing. I believe negotiation is for two-way co-creation to maximise mutual benefits.

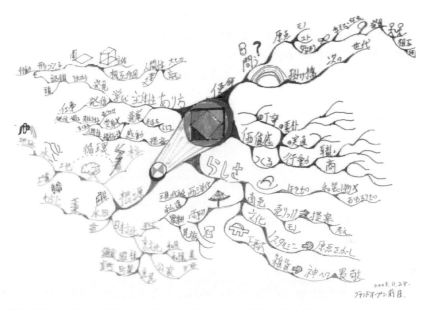

Mind Map by Seijo Naito used to help him untangle the threads

The above case study demonstrates that when creating Mind Maps you can 'listen' as well as take notes and present information, and this will help your concentration on the matter in hand before, during and after negotiations.

Creating Mind Maps at all stages of negotiations can be a contributory factor in sealing a deal. By their very nature they work with your brain to interconnect the keywords, colours, shapes and images as you project and respond to negotiating scenarios. Don't worry if your Mind Map gets messy in the process – you can tidy it up afterwards if it needs to be distributed to colleagues.

Mind Maps can be excellent guides to 'work in progress' in business, but they can also form a key element of formal or informal presentations when clearly and legibly created. The next chapter will demonstrate how Mind Maps can form part of a business presentation by an individual and be used to guide others through your own personal thoughts while also providing a tool for discussion of ideas or to find a solution to corporate problems.

Mind Maps For Business Online

Sometimes it can be daunting to have to negotiate a deal with a prospect or supplier. Use the iMindMap templates to make the process much easier ensuring you see all of the options and gambits that might be played. You will also find articles, tutorials, tips and how-to guides relating to negotiations at www.MindMapsForBusiness.com.

Mind Mapping successful presentations

When using a Mind Map you are always operating from one sheet, so you can tell your audience what you plan to say, you can say it with confidence and then you can recap to demonstrate you have proved your point.

RAYMOND KEENE OBE, chess Grandmaster

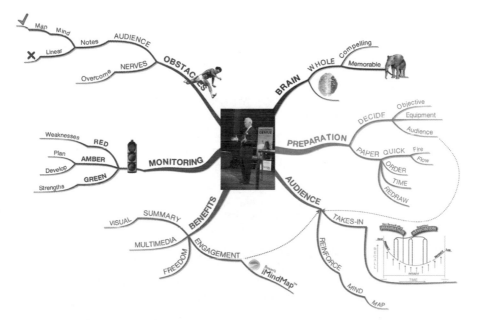

Mind Map summary for Chapter 6

Most businesses will need to make a presentation at some stage or another; to some it is a key part of sealing a deal, selling their ideas or products, to others it may be an occasional thing simply to let other colleagues or board members know how a company is performing and what the future holds. Whatever your reasons for making a presentation, to achieve the result you want the presentation needs to be prepared and executed with care and thought.

Tony Buzan presenting on stage

All presentations are essentially brain-based: the presenter's brain 'talks' to the brains of the audience members. It is brain-to-brain communication. This may be the first time you have heard it described as such; you need to understand this perspective or run the risk of using only half your brain – and having less than half the impact on your audience.

Using Mind Maps to plan and guide you through a presentation will enable your brain to combine the logical with the imaginative, and thereby to communicate fully with the brains of your audience members. By preparing, supporting and reviewing your presentation using Mind Maps, you will both overcome any natural anxieties about getting up and speaking in public and deliver a memorable 'whole-brained' speech.

Whole-brained presentations

If you can grasp the concept of brains communicating with brains, you will need to remember the 'brain of two halves' concept (see Chapter 1). The right hemisphere processes intellectual areas such as rhythm, spatial awareness, mental manipulation of whole units, imagination, daydreaming, colour and dimension, while the left hemisphere appears dominant in a different but equally powerful range of mental skills: words, logic, numbers, sequence, linearity, analysis and lists.

While a professional presentation must be based on informative, well-organised, factual, step-by-step material, it needs other facets to make it compelling, such as a variation in pacing, articulate body language, and plenty of vivid visual imagery. That is because audience members tend to focus on these aspects as much as on the words delivered. You need to tap into the billions of neural interactions firing between each half of your brain.

So, if you want to make your presentation engaging and memorable you must use your 'whole brain' – mixing imagery and intuition with logic and analysis.

How to prepare your presentation using Mind Maps

Creating a Mind Map when preparing for a presentation or speech involves virtually the same process as Mind Mapping for note-taking and organising (see page 68). First you need to identify the essential elements of your subject in a Mind Map, then finalise your Mind Map to encapsulate all the key elements and associations of that presentation.

Begin by deciding on your objective for the presentation: what is it that you want to achieve? Next, decide what form your presentation should take, how visual it should be and what equipment you need to get your ideas across – perhaps by PowerPoint, posters, or by demonstrating the item you are selling or proposing. Take into consideration, too, your audience – whether it is an informal or formal situation, how well you know the people you are presenting to, and therefore how you might present your ideas to best appeal to them. Think through the structure of your speech and the order in which you want to discuss ideas. All these factors can be successfully mind mapped to give you a clear picture of how your presentation might unfold, giving you the confidence of being well prepared to speak.

The virtue of using a Mind Map to prepare a speech is that the presenter is constantly stimulated by the branching trees of ideas to unearth new and more daring thoughts, while at the same time the keywords and images ensure that, in the actual delivery, no major point is overlooked.

The Mind Map is a highly focused tool in this context. The fact that the whole process is laid out on a single page has obvious benefits during the presentation, in that it becomes possible to inform the audience in advance about the structure and key points of your speech without turning or shuffling pages. Presenting this way means you bypass the danger of linear notes – that you might finish speaking simply where the notes stop; in essence a random moment which is often determined by chronology rather than meaning.

Assuming that the speaker or lecturer has complete command of his or her subject, the keywords act as a catalyst for enthusiasm and interconnected ideas instead of a dry recitation of facts, often determined by dates or a list of bullet-point findings. If the speaker does not have a perfect grasp of the subject, linear notes simply make it worse. For giving a verbal lecture or presentation, the Mind Map acts like a helm to navigate through the main oceans of the presentation.

Getting it down on paper

As with other applications of Mind Maps, start with a central image or keyword that encapsulates the subject of your presentation.

From that core visual do a quick-fire Mind-Map burst of ideas that spring to mind which are in any way connected to the subject you have chosen. From these you can then select appropriate Basic Ordering Ideas. Let your mind range freely, adding items of information or points you wish to make wherever they seem most relevant on your Mind Map. As we have already seen, there is no limit to the number of branches and sub-branches that can radiate from your Basic Ordering Ideas.

At this stage you should write as quickly as possible, skipping over any areas that cause you difficulty, especially particular topics or links. In this way you will create a much greater flow, and you can always return to the problem areas later.

If you come up against 'presenter's block', doing another Mind Map will help you overcome it. In many cases just drawing the central image will get your mind going again, playing and freewheeling around the topic of your speech. If you get blocked once more, simply add new lines branching from the keywords and images you have so far generated, and your brain's natural gestalt or 'completing tendency' will fill in the blank spaces with new words and images.

Remember the brain's infinite capacity for association and allow all your thoughts to flow, especially the ones you may have been dismissing as 'absurd'. Such blocks will disappear as soon as you realise they are not actually created by your brain's inability to connect, but by an underlying fear of failure and a misunderstanding of the way the brain works. Fear of failure in presentations is one of the biggest challenges in the workplace.

Look again at your quick-fire Mind Map, organise your main branches and sub-branches, adding codes (i.e. colours, symbols, or both) to indicate where you wish to insert slides or videos, as well to indicate particular cross-references and examples.

Now consider the order in which you wish to present your main branches and number them accordingly.

Finally, allocate to each branch an appropriate length of time you wish to speak on that particular point. As each keyword will take up at least one minute of your presentation, probably a little more, it's a good idea to restrict your Mind Map to a maximum of 35 keywords and images for a maximum one-hour speech.

If you like, you can now redraw a neater 'edited' and reordered or refined Mind Map presentation of your draft version. This will reinforce the memory through the repetition of recreating and also, being neater, make it easier to follow during your actual presentation.

A well-organised Mind Map should provide you with all the main subdivisions of your presentation, the key points to be mentioned, and the way in which those points relate to each other. Now you can just follow your own instincts.

Understanding what your audience takes in – recall during learning

If your content is to be engaging for your audience, understanding a bit about the recall during learning (listening) process will help you get a head start when presenting. After all, you want your audience to *remember* your presentation, so understanding something of the nature of memory can be extremely helpful.

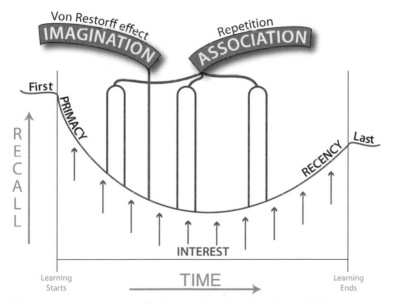

This chart shows the Von Restorff effect, a memorisation effect which demonstrates when recall is at its highest

'Recall during learning' is a term used to explain the nature of what we absorb through our senses and what actually 'sticks' in the memory. During your presentation your audience will be 'learning' and they will remember more at the beginning and at the end and less in the middle, where their memories will 'sag'. They will also remember any parts throughout that stand out to them, and any parts that have some link or association to other parts of the content, or to your internal 'database'.

The patterns that occur through recall during learning can be visualised through this diagram that shows the Von Restorff effect, which is a memorisation effect named after the psychologist who discovered it, Hedwig Von Restorff. If you imagine that this is a presentation, notice that at the beginning and at the end the recalled amount is high. The beginning is known as the 'primacy effect' and the ending is called the 'recency effect'.

The recall during learning curve shows that there is a drop in the middle of the learning process or, in this case, your presentation. In the main, the only elements of the middle part of a presentation that are remembered clearly are the interesting, outstanding ones or the elements that have some sort of link to other points at either end of the presentation. The elements that stand out are often sparked by the imagination.

The other effective technique for aiding recall is association – creating links with something else during a presentation, or with the listener personally. The more repetitive these associative points are, the more the audience will be able to remember them. Taking note of this, for example in your introduction where you have the benefit of the primacy effect, the prime association is not you and the information; it's the information and the audience. A projected Mind Map or other visual image, sharing a joke, or involving the audience in some way will immediately capture the listeners' attention.

Similarly, if you want to sum up with impact, don't end with 'That's all I have to say, um, thank, er, you'. Instead use the mnemonic device of repetition, repetition, repetition to help the brain remember what it is you are saying. If you finish without taking advantage of the recency effect, an extremely large and crucial section of your presentation will be unnecessarily forgotten.

Just as you gave your audience an outline of your talk during your introduction, be sure to restate your main points one more time in your conclusion. Create a punchy conclusion that summarises all the main points you talked about in your presentation. Try to do this as creatively as possible – perhaps through a final story, some interaction with your audience, or as the solution to a puzzle or riddle you told during the middle of your talk.

Your presentation Mind Map should now reflect the recall during learning curve and should contain everything you want your audience to take away from your presentation: information, inspiration, enjoyment, happiness …

And remember to use the recency effect to its full potential to guarantee that your principal message will be remembered long after the audience has left the auditorium.

A key factor in maintaining the interest of your audience during a presentation concerns timing. Do not talk for too long; many presentations go on and on, giving too much detail that could be better given as part of a question and answer session. Tell your audience at the beginning that you will happily answer questions at the end if they want you to expand on points further, which will allow you to keep your presentation short and simple.

Reinforcing your presentation with a Mind Map

The art of good presentation involves understanding the operation of memory and recall in your audience. The Mind Map is itself a mnemonic – a memory tool that can work both for you and for the audience. For example, a great advantage of the Mind Map is that you can project it on screen from time to time in your presentation for everyone to see. Being colourful and visual, the Mind Map becomes a powerful memory jogger and signpost of what you're going to say, as you say it, and after you've said it.

Tony Buzan presenting on stage

Remember that Mind Maps work in the same way that your brain does: by image and association, thereby by their very nature they organically aid memory. Therefore, while you are preparing a Mind Map of your presentation you will be etching that Mind Map in your head, and the memorisation will be done in a subconscious way while you are creating it. As a result, you will find that very often you don't need the completed piece of paper in front of you because everything that's on it is there inside your head.

New Zealand Defence Force brief to troops

The New Zealand Defence Force (NZDF) has peacekeepers deployed to assist in areas of conflict around the world. Some locations have animals and plants, diseases and pests not present in New Zealand, such as foot and mouth, fruit flies, or invasive weed species (Siam weed). If any of these were brought back to New Zealand the primary-industry based economy, environment and export market opportunities could be threatened.

The Ministry of Agriculture and Forestry, Biosecurity New Zealand (MAFBNZ) sends inspectors overseas as part of the military Force Extraction Team (FET) to brief troops, supervise packing and inspect personal baggage and equipment for those returning to New Zealand (RTNZ). This manages the biological risks offshore and facilitates arrival formalities.

One challenge is to ensure that all inspectors provide a consistent five-minute briefing presentation. Talks are given to small units in the field, in unfamiliar environments, without visual aids and often under tense conditions.

The Mind Map developed to assist inspectors is used to ensure that the message:

- is presented in a logical sequence;
- covers all the points that need to be conveyed;
- supports the less confident public speakers.

This method of briefing improves compliance. As a result, a peacekeeper almost always presents his or her gear in a clean and dry condition. Disputes about the requirement to remove laces, pack frames or dismantle webbing to aid inspection are minimised. Fair warning has been given to all personnel that the Australian Quarantine Inspection Service (AQIS) may conduct checks if troops transit through Australia. Everyone knows that spot checks will be carried out using x-rays or detector dogs on arrival home in New Zealand. Surprises are thus avoided.

If the inspector is detained elsewhere, is sick or unavailable when the brief is to be given, a Defence Force officer or NCO untrained in biosecurity can present the information adequately using the Mind Map as a model. The winner is New Zealand's biosecurity.

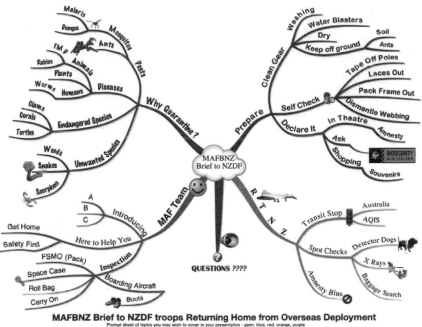

MAFBNZ Brief to NZDF troops Returning Home from Overseas Deployment
Prompt sheet of topics you may wish to cover in your presentation - geen, blue, red, orange, purple
Version 2.2

This is a Mind Map template for a brief to the New Zealand Defence Force on troops returning home from deployment
Source: With thanks to Jaimie Baird for supplying the above case study, **www.biosecurity. govt.nz/biosec/org/history/updates**.

Key benefits of Mind Maps for presentations over written notes

Preparing your presentation using a Mind Map allows you to use a greater range of your cortical skills.

Having your ideas written down clearly on a single piece of paper, rather than reams of pages, means that you don't have to refer to your notes as often, allowing you to speak freely and increase that all-important eye contact with the audience. Equally, Mind Maps are also less restrictive in a physical sense in that the speaker can move around while he talks, if he wishes, and is free to make physical gestures to reinforce major points, work a computer presentation or demonstrate equipment without having to hold onto notes at the same time. This improved contact and connection between the speaker and his or her audience also increases their involvement in the presentation.

In the same way, written language is very different from spoken language. Grammatically correct written language is inappropriate for a spoken presentation and will almost certainly induce extreme boredom in the audience. A Mind Map gives the presenter the perfect balance between the spontaneity of natural speech and the structure of worked-out ideas. This powerful combination is the key to effective (and confident) presentations and inevitably results in a more memorable, effective and enjoyable performance for both the speaker and the audience.

Mind Maps allow you to think around a subject, both in the planning stages and during the presentation itself. They also allow you more flexibility in your delivery of ideas than a preconceived script, which enables you to adapt your presentation to the needs of the audience confidently and to time it precisely when planning it, and to alter or expand key points as you present them, based on the response and feedback you are experiencing from your audience. For example, if your remarks are met with confusion you are able to better explain yourself or ask for questions from the audience without fear of losing your way through the presentation, or if you can see that a point is not holding their interest, you can swiftly move on without having to flick through pages of notes to find the next section. A prepared speech is always 'out of date' from the moment you start speaking; it does not allow the speaker to adjust to the audience's immediate needs or to adapt in response to points made by, say, a previous speaker.

If you are delivering a presentation that is supported by iMindMaps, you can take the audience on a visual interactive journey through your ideas and can combine or 'meld' the iMindMaps seamlessly into other interactive presentation software. The joy of delivering your presentation from a single piece of paper will also be felt by your audience – generally, unless your presentation is utterly riveting, after about 20 minutes the attention of the people in the first 30 rows tends to be less on the content of the speech than on how many pages of it are left!

Presenting with multimedia

Research has shown that people respond better to visual presentations than verbal ones and remember almost two-thirds more of the points discussed up to 3 days later. So it follows that a successful presentation should involve some sort of visual device to support the ideas being presented. Most of us use multimedia when we make presentations, whether PowerPoint slides or other audio and visual aids. Of course, these can be a blessing and a curse; audiences are familiar, perhaps too familiar, with multimedia presentations, and the danger is always that the medium might obscure the message rather than convey it.

Used well, though, multimedia can truly enrich what we say, adding a wonderfully vibrant visual and creative dimension to our presentations. Used badly, they distract the audience from the main focus – you and your message – and can test patience if the technology suddenly 'switches off'. It is certainly worth considering embellishing your presentation with multimedia, but remember not to rely on such things and not to use them as a prop to hide behind – they should simply reinforce what you say.

Summing up

Using a Mind Map in your presentation is a superb way to add a visual element to what you say. It can be used at the beginning to map out what you are going to cover, then be referred to throughout as an anchor. It's also a neat way to summarise your key points and ideas at the end, so that your audience goes away with everything still in their mind.

iMindMap software has been specifically developed to be used in presentations and has all sorts of features that make it highly effective as a presentation tool. These include expanding and collapsing branches, focusing in and out on a particular branch, exporting to PowerPoint or Keynote, exporting your Mind Map and converting it into a fully structured presentation, and putting your Mind Map onto one slide and animating it. If you use software such as iMindMap intelligently and link it in with what you are saying, not as a sideshow, you will capture the audience's attention. (For a full tutorial on how to use iMindMap in your presentation, visit **www.imindmap.com**.)

Mind map to monitor your presentation skills

A great way to monitor your continuous improvement in presentations and get into a positive feedback loop is to create a performance-coaching-style Mind Map which can be very successful for monitoring your progress and improvement (see also Chapter 5). For example:

- **Red branches** – Mind map the areas where you need to improve – your weak techniques and skills.

- **Green branches** – Mind map your strengths and the skills for which you were praised.

- **Amber branches** – This is where you would mind map your development needs.

Copy and use the performance-coaching Mind Map below to mark your feedback from each of your presentations. (Or visit **www.imindmap.com** to find a template.)

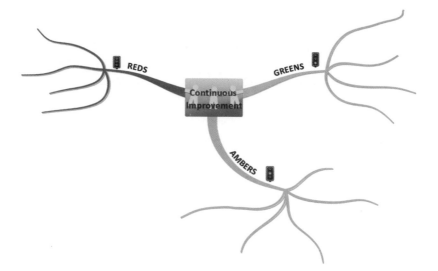

A Mind Map template showing how to monitor improvement in presentation skills using red, amber and green branches

Start with the green branch and to it add your skills, techniques and presentation qualities that your audience commented on positively. While it may be hard to dwell on the negatives, it is important that you review the areas that you and/or your audience felt could be improved. Be honest and define the skills and parts of your presentation that were seen to be weak and mind map them on the red branches.

Finally, you need to look forward and mind map your development needs – things that you can work on and strengthen for your next presentation. These areas for improvement should be marked on the amber branches. Really think about this part of your Mind Map, as this is the most valuable segment for you because here you can set yourself goals and a clear path forward.

When you have finished your Mind Map, print it out and keep it close by you, perhaps even on your wall. Aim to continually work on your development needs wherever possible, and refer to the Mind Map every time you prepare a presentation.

After each presentation, create another improvement Mind Map, based on your original one, in order to keep a record of how you are progressing. You will find that the more presentations you do, the more feedback you receive, and the more you review yourself, the better your presentations will become.

Beat presentation nerves

For some, just the thought of giving a presentation sends them into a cold sweat. Often this can be the fear of drying up mid speech, losing their way, not being prepared, or anxiety that questions might be asked that they will struggle to answer when put on the spot. Creating Mind Maps that encompass all these issues will help you combat your fears, and this will leave you relaxed and ready to speak, which is important as the best presentations are those given by people who appear to be at ease and are being themselves.

Talking to your audience should be as natural as talking to friends and family. If you are relaxed and don't try to wear a mask you will find you act more naturally, words will flow more easily and you will have more confidence. Your speech will be more conversational, relaxed and smoother, too.

If you slip up, don't panic; making a mistake is part of the natural flow of conversation and you should be able to correct it and move on; rather than freezing when you make a mistake, just laugh it off. Make your audience feed off your comfort with yourself and continue on with your presentation. Take a deep breath, pause and say something like, 'I've become so engrossed in the concept I've forgotten the next point. Let me go back to my Mind Map. Ah, yes ...'. Bring your audience back to the Mind Map (by bringing it back to view on screen) and take your time to find your trail of thought again.

Use Mind Maps to overcome presentation anxieties

Here's how you can use a Mind Map to overcome natural anxieties. First, create a Mind Map about the things that worry you while presenting.

Your central idea has already been created for you – 'Fears while presenting', so from this you need to draw your main branches which will carry your uppermost anxieties when presenting. Make sure each main branch represents a mistake you are afraid of making. For example, 'forgetting'.

Once you have your set of main branches you can now create secondary or child branches that drill down into the details. For example, 'forgetting' (main branch) leads to 'change' on the second branch, which leads to 'slides' on the third branch (see figure overleaf).

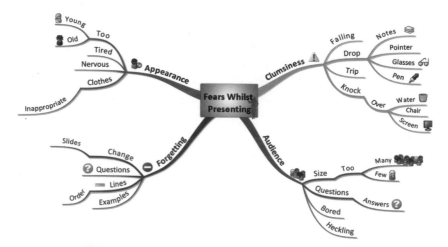

A Mind Map showing how to deal with fears while presenting

Anxiety and stress may manifest themselves in sweating, stuttering, trembling hands, fidgeting, increased heart rate, nausea, dry mouth, dizziness and shortness of breath. Your Mind Map can explore the symptoms you experience while presenting, looking both at the physical and mental ones. This will help you start to build up a picture of your attitudes and the consequences.

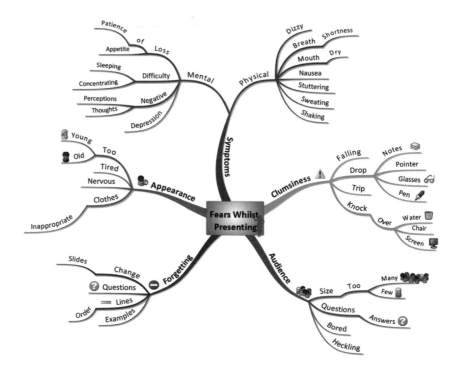

A Mind Map with further branches to map your fears while making a presentation

Here is a Mind Map you can adapt to help you overcome the fear of failure.

Use this template to address your own issues. Draw the final main branch and label it 'overcome'. Now think of all the things you can do to fight your fear of presenting – things that will help you to be yourself. For example, laughing. Add all your ideas via secondary (or child) branches and look at your Mind Map whenever you are preparing a presentation and just before you give one. In between, work on the issues you have highlighted and see if you can reduce, if not overcome, your anxieties.

Mind Mapping presentations – the audience perspective

Mind Maps enable you to create a record of both the 'big picture' and the important details on a single sheet. The same is true if you are taking notes as an audience member at a presentation, seminar, lecture, briefing or public speech.

By its very nature, the linear presentation of standard notes prevents the brain from making associations, thus counteracting creativity and memory. Our current note-making and -taking systems therefore produce ever-diminishing returns. What we need is a system that produces *increasing* returns. The Mind Map, as a visual tool and one that can be viewed at a glance on a single sheet, is also instantaneous and abounding with keywords, colour and associations, and as such allows you to tune into a clearer, more natural and more efficient way of using your brain, which in turn gives you a positive feedback loop.

With information overload in the workplace being all too common, this is even more vital. Moreover, the irrational urge to be 'completist' means we end up scribbling copious notes and so miss the all-important facial gestures and body language of the speaker. We become absorbed in the time-consuming habit of making notes on notes in an attempt to discover the ever more elusive essence of what has just been said. The harder we work, the less we progress, because we are unwittingly working against ourselves and wasting time.

Standard notes have less than 10 per cent of the notes themselves as keywords. So when you are making linear notes you are wasting 90 per cent of your time making them; then you waste another 90 per cent of your time rereading them. All that is necessary for recall are the speaker's keywords, which, with the imagination and associative links of the Mind Map, are inbuilt.

Mind Mapping a seminar – the audience perspective

As an audience member you too can use Mind Maps for creative note-taking to get the best from a presentation.

In this example, Lim Choon Boo, Principal Lecturer at the Singapore School of Engineering, made a Mind Map of a recent speech given by Mr Lim Siong Guan, at the Institution of Engineers Singapore (IES) Charles Rudd Distinguished Annual Lecture on 16 September 2008.

Choon Boo was inspired by what Mr Lim would have said to people who tell us that we can't do it – 'Just ignore them, as they do not want us to succeed' – and drew this Mind Map accordingly. Mr Lim Siong Guan is Chairman of the Singapore Economic Development Board, Director of Temasek Holdings Pte Ltd, and Board Member of the National Research Foundation. Mr Lim is also an Adjunct Professor in the Lee Kuan Yew School of Public Policy at the National University of Singapore, instructing on leadership and change management in the public sector.

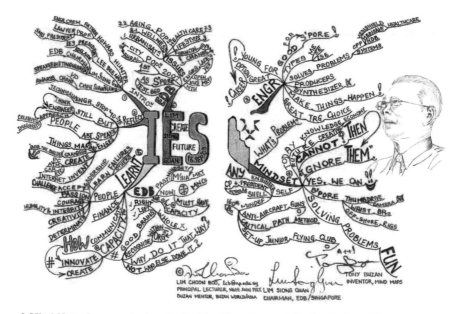

A Mind Map of a speech given by Mr Lim Siong Guan, at the Institution of Engineers Singapore (IES)

Using Mind Maps as part of your presentation adds a very powerful and memorable visual aid for your audience. With iMindMap software, which has presentation tools built in, the process is made even easier, and the visuals can help to aid memory and therefore your audience's interest in your presentation.

A presentation is just one part of running a business and pitching for a deal. Once you've secured that all-important contract it is important for good future relations with clients to ensure the smooth running of your business. Successful project management in part requires good organisation (see Chapter 4); there are other key elements involved too. Once more, this is an area of business in which Mind Maps can be an effective tool, and Chapter 7 will explain exactly how.

 The Buzan Organisation's research shows you forget 80 per cent of what you have learnt within 24 hours, and the most important time to revisit the information to ensure it is retained is one hour after you have first absorbed it. Take a break for 60 minutes and then visit www.MindMapsForBusiness.com to start applying what you have just learnt to create your next presentation.

Mind Mapping for effective project management

I have to order it or it just doesn't work for me. And the Mind Map is one of the tools that I use. When it comes to defining or creating something, Mind Maps give me a head start.

SAM BROOKS, design engineer, Boeing

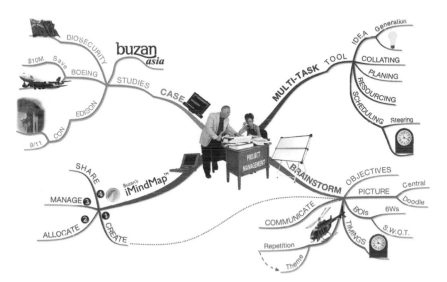

Mind Map summary for Chapter 7

Planning and managing a project, whether one that is long term or short term, can swallow up reams of paper and paperwork – not to mention time. Just setting up the project proposal may involve extensive research and reporting in written, graphic and oral form. Mind Maps are a superb tool for collating all this information and using it as the project develops, as they reflect both the changeable nature of a project and the elasticity of the brain in coping with the ebb and flow of setting a project on course and guiding it to a successful outcome.

Mind Maps are especially useful for planning events, product development and sales planning, and iMindMaps can now be used for and integrated with project management processes, from gathering ideas and planning to scheduling, managing and sharing.

Multi-task tool for a multi-task skill

There is no doubt that project management is a demanding combination of tasks and skills. Among them is the process of ideas generation (see also Chapter 9) and collating the elements to form your project; this is followed by detailed planning and resource allocation, and finally scheduling and steering. All these stages can be time-consuming, stressful, and most of all fragile. Forget one task and your project could crumble as everything will be out of sync.

Mind Mapping all these details is a natural way of using links and associations creatively to get everything down in front of you in a coherent fashion. For instance, during the research phase you can use Mind Maps to organise your notes from source material, write up research results, and organise and integrate your ideas as they emerge. A Mind Map can then form the basis of your project. Like a mind-mapped to-do list or weekly diary, projects created in this way are likely to be much better structured, more focused and more original than those based on the laborious methods of standard linear note-taking (with all their drafting and redrafting).

Using computer Mind Mapping allows you to take the process even further: you can link standard project management software under a Mind Map umbrella and also integrate and share your Mind Maps with colleagues and teams using the standard embedded project processes (see also page 124).

How to get the most out of project management with Mind Maps

You can use Mind Maps for project management in two different ways:

● To brainstorm and evaluate different strategies and objectives (see also Chapter 9).

- To make a 'work breakdown structure' once the main objective of the project has become clear. This would be the analysis of one main goal: write the main objective of the project in the middle and break it down into sub-objectives, then keep doing that for each sub-objective until you end with actions. These actions are the ones that need to be planned and monitored.

The largest project Mind Map

The illustration below shows Dr Mike Stanley, Project Leader at the Boeing Aircraft Corporation in Seattle, in front of a 25-foot-long Mind Map he created to condense an aircraft design and engineering manual. This enabled a project team of 100 senior aeronautical engineers to learn in a few weeks what had previously taken a few years. There were also considerable cost savings. Mike Stanley said:

The use of Mind Mapping [was] an integral part of my Quality Improvement programme here at Boeing. This programme provided savings of over $10 million for my organisation (ten times our goal). We developed a unique application of mind-mapping techniques to identify Quality Improvement projects here at Boeing. Within one month, over 500 projects were identified which represent millions of dollars of potential cost savings.

Dr Stanley with the 25-foot-long Boeing Aircraft Mind Map

Mind Mapping the Buzan Asia Project

Another use of project management by planning, running and communicating with Mind Maps helped Buzan Asia start up eight national centres in less than 24 months. From late 2006 to mid 2008, Buzan Asia established centres in Indonesia, the Philippines, India, Hong Kong, Singapore, Thailand, Korea and Malaysia. Henry Toi takes up the story:

I was trained as an engineer, but because of my deep interest in finance I had also planned to work in the finance industry. Upon graduation, even though it was a recession year, I landed a job at the central bank in Singapore, having competed with more than 500 applicants. It was a fascinating job, working with ministers, top civil servants, senior bankers and bank owners and dealing in billion-dollar transactions. Nevertheless, I knew it was temporary. My final destination was to begin a business of my own. In 1992, after spending seven years in banking, I started my business. By 1996, it had become the fastest growing retail chain, Nurture Craft.

We were establishing franchise outlets on an average of one every three months. By that time we had 14 outlets stretching from Penang to Singapore. But somehow it was not as satisfying as I had imagined it would be. I had imagined a business that was positive, uplifting, meaningful and fulfilling. Then came the Asian financial crisis. Almost overnight, the outlets suffered price shocks. Asian currencies were devaluing so fast that by the time a cargo of goods leaving the UK reached Malaysia, the cost would have become higher than the retail price at which we were selling. Milk powder prices on the supermarket shelves doubled within a week. The financial and industrial markets collapsed. In my search for a re-imagined meaningful business, rereading a well-worn copy of *Use Your Head* by Tony Buzan helped to re-engineer the rebuilding of the business. I was so convinced about the power and applicability of Mind Maps that I decided to become a master instructor of this powerful technique.

Birthing the plan

The combined effects of training in the correct use of Mind Maps and the re-imagined new business ignited a vision for me of a 'mentally literate' Asia. At the turn of the twenty-first century Asia was still in mental slumber. Three billion people with little or no knowledge of how to use their heads! The mission was clear: I had to put in place a sustainable way to make Asia 'mentally literate'. Mind mapping my way through the research process, brainstorming and planning uncovered the solution; it was to establish

The Buzan Asia team celebrating the biggest Mind Map in the world and achieving 6000 Mind Mappers taught in Singapore for 2008

self-supporting Buzan Centres in every major city in Asia, where Buzan methods of teaching, learning and thinking would be taught.

The journey began with sharing the vision with the initial instructors in Singapore. I called for several meetings and had many working sessions, naturally assisted and facilitated by the use of Mind Maps in discussing plans for Buzan Centres.

The next step was to build the corporate structure of the company. I chose Hong Kong as the corporate base, as there were no instructors in Hong Kong and it also offered the additional benefit of being the gateway to China. The next three years were spent building a strong base of Asian instructors. They came from Hong Kong, Malaysia, Indonesia, India, China, the Philippines, Singapore, Taiwan and Thailand. As we intended to establish Buzan Centres in every major city in Asia, we made it a part of the Buzan Licensed Instructor course that each participant Mind Map their vision for Mind Maps in their own country. From these Mind Maps we were able to identify and select Buzan Centre national directors. Mind Maps are excellent for understanding vision in broad and detailed terms.

Meetings of minds with Mind Maps

After the stage of shortlisting the national directors, the ongoing discussions over the phone were mind mapped for clarity and accountability. Each conversation was mind mapped and referred to in subsequent teleconferences. Mind Maps facilitated the building of the business.

Today at meetings within Buzan Centres minutes are taken in Mind Maps, which have the dual qualities of clarity and efficiency. With the launch of iMindMap software all minutes are taken in iMindMap. This gave us the added advantage of ease of distribution using emails. Review of minutes is also much easier as it can be exported to Microsoft PowerPoint and therefore integrated with other PowerPoint presentations.

Tony Buzan launching the Buzan Centre Pune

Each meeting is prefaced with an overview of the agenda in Mind Map form. These help us to manage the time spent on each agenda item as well as to see the interconnectedness in the items being discussed. Many enjoyable hours were spent at meetings where Mind Maps guided our collective thoughts. Some of these were meetings on strategic directions, such as deciding if Buzan Asia should be built as a distribution-dominant company or a product-dominant company. At every meeting, Mind Maps helped to illuminate our thinking.

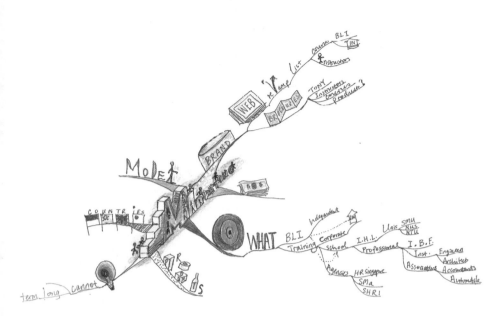

Example of a Mind Map used to guide planning for Buzan Asia's business

The mind's 'drawing board'

The priority in project management is to make sure you include everything that needs to be considered before you start getting into the detail. Using a Mind Map as a white space thinking tool allows you to do just that. You can see the whole picture, which allows you to see the answers to such questions as, 'What needs to happen to make this happen?'

As your thinking expands, so does your Mind Map, as you extend the branches and sub-branches from the core image. Most traditional project management software is not brain-friendly: it is still reliant on spreadsheet and word-processing software – which means an over-dependence on lists. Lists do not allow your brain and creativity to flow and, critically, do not succinctly address the core question: 'What do I need to do to make this project happen?'

Mind Mapping a project

First off, think of a stimulating central picture that encapsulates your project. Put this image in the centre of your page and let your brain start to associate freely from there. If your mind goes blank, disconnect from your project and start doodling, colouring or drawing in your central picture. By doing this, the chances are that your brain will start to feed you fresh associations. When that happens, stop drawing and capture the ideas that come.

Just as with Mind Mapping for note-taking (see Chapter 4), another very helpful technique for getting the planning for a project under way is by the use of templates. Start from Basic Ordering Ideas (BOIs), for example the 6Ws of sustainable corporate growth (who, what, when, where, why, how) or SWOT (strengths, weaknesses, opportunities and threats).

Use a sheet big enough to give you space to lay out as many associations as possible, adding your ideas to the branches that triggered them for a maximum of 15 minutes. Giving yourself a limited amount of time to do this helps free your mind from habitual thinking schemes, and this will encourage original ideas and sometimes seemingly absurd ones. Do not judge the quality of the ideas generated and do not dismiss them on the spot; an idea which seems absurd will often be the seed of a very valuable idea. If an idea that pops up seems 'irrelevant' to you, put it as a secondary idea on a branch without a BOI. Keep doing that for every apparently 'irrelevant' idea that your brain gives you. In the end, your brain will give meaning to this branch. Make sure to put no more than one word per branch; that will give each key idea more freedom, and your brain more possibilities for association.

Take a short break after 20 or 30 minutes. The human brain performs better when it is given regular opportunities to relax. These small interruptions help the brain either to integrate the ideas already captured, or to incubate new ones. Just before or after that break take a moment to 'helicopter' out of your Mind Map and look for repetitions. Rather than being avoided, these apparent 'redundancies' should be encouraged because they very often hold the key to a mind-shift.

If the same concept appears several times in your Mind Map, highlight it or frame it in a three-dimensional shape. You may well decide to start a new Mind Map with this repeated concept in the centre. Very often this repeated idea is your brain discovering a major new theme, and it can lead to a paradigm shift in your reasoning. To emphasise it, box it in each time it occurs, and if it occurs many times, give it extra dimension and visual depth and highlight it throughout the Mind Map, as this will help you discover significant and original topics in your thinking.

Finish your Mind Map and then communicate it to others. Their comments – which are the result of associations made by other brains – might lead you to new ideas or, again, to changes of reasoning. Add all these to your Mind Map.

A real-life example of a project for interpersonal training skills for Deloitte Belgium is given opposite. This Mind Map also served as a handout for participants in the training. Another Mind Map, also from Belgium, shows a project involving Stabilo – notice the branches that have been ticked off.

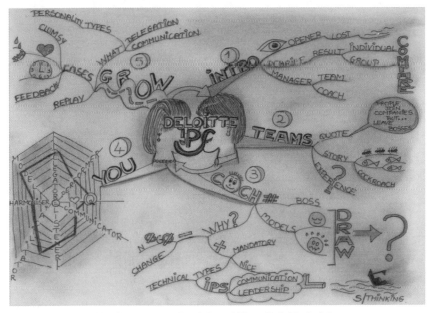

Mind Map created for interpersonal training skills at Deloitte Belgium

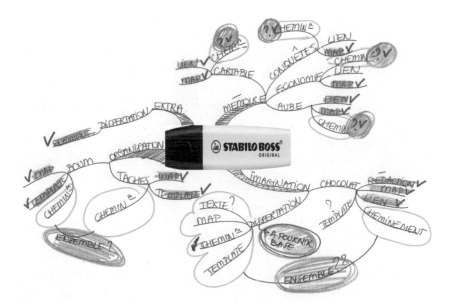

Mind Map for Stabilo project

Biosecurity history project outline

Focus, focus, focus. Even small and low-risk projects need a plan. The plan should describe the project scope, it should identify required outcomes, and it should detail resources and time-frames. The project plan can easily balloon in to many pages of uninspiring narrative with seemingly little relationship to results.

Project paperwork is a management requirement. It is rarely read by participants and never seen by the wider community. It is most necessary and cannot be avoided or totally replaced by a Mind Map.

In an effort to demonstrate an application for mind mapping, but at the same time provide the project plan outline on a single page, a Mind Map of the Ministry of Agriculture and Forestry's Biosecurity New Zealand history project was developed. Goals are shown by 'smiley faces' and a big red tick is shown upon completion. The Mind Map provides visibility and encourages accountability. It aids presentations and helps to explain the project to outsiders. It keeps the team on track and it achieves focus. Producing it in an iMindMap also allowed amendment to reflect change.

This is believed to be the first Mind Map displayed publicly on a New Zealand Government webpage. For those interested in following this project, visit **www.biosecurity.govt.nz/history** and click on Updates to open the Project Plan Overview.

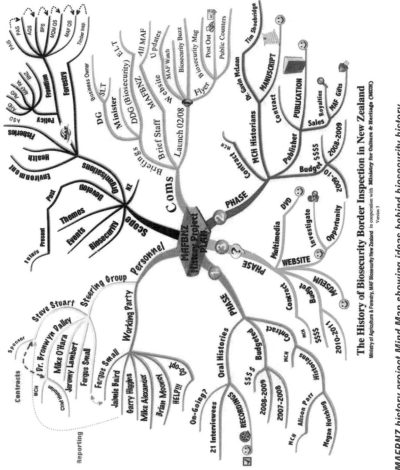

The History of Biosecurity Border Inspection in New Zealand

Ministry of Agriculture & Forestry, MAF Biosecurity New Zealand in cooperation with Ministry for Culture & Heritage (MCH)
Version 3

A MAFBNZ history project Mind Map showing ideas behind biosecurity history

Computer Mind Maps and project management

If you prefer a technological approach to project management and you want to be able to produce clear, non-hand-written Mind Maps that can be easily passed around colleagues at the touch of the mouse, the iMindMap program can do it for you. The iMindMap's Project Management System integrates Mind Maps into a business project management tool.

Mind Maps can be created on the computer very simply (see Chapter 3 for more information), and here are a few simple steps for how to mind map a project – on screen and on paper.

Step 1: Create

Start by creating a New Mind Map with your project name as your central idea.

It is best to start your Mind Map in Speed Mind Map Mode to get your ideas down quickly. If you are doing this on computer, iMindMap will organise your thoughts systematically; go to 'Mode' to select Speed Mind Map and then choose an 'Auto Layout' style for your Mind Map – you have a choice of ten different settings ranging from Linear to Organic to Radial.

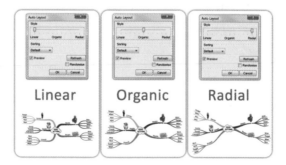

Next, as with all Mind Maps, you need to brainstorm your project and let your mind wander through all the various avenues of ideas and issues. A good place to start would be to create main branches for all the different areas involved in your project. Each main branch in your Mind Map represents an area of the project and forms a Summary Task within your project.

Imagine you are putting together an external training course: using your Mind Map, consider all the different resources and challenges involved. Your main branches could be: Course content; Course materials; Venue; Equipment; Attendees.

Training Day - 12th January 2009

From your main branches or areas, continue to mind map all the different elements that will be involved in your project; let your brain think 'radiantly' and make its own instantaneous connections and associations.

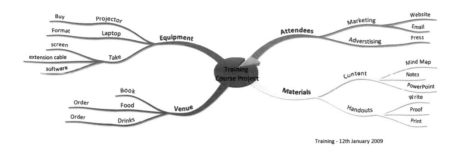

Training - 12th January 2009

Step 2: Allocate

Ensure that every task that will form part of your project appears on the final 'child branch' of a major branch. These child branches will form the tasks within your Task Table and Gantt Chart. While each end child branch represents a Task, its parent(s) will be Summary Task(s).

Continue until you have added all areas and tasks to your mind map. This process of splitting your ideas into different areas and then allowing your brain to think by associations and connections should culminate in a project overview that contains *all* of your project tasks in an easy-to-view one-page document.

If you are using a computer program to generate your Mind Map, once you have your completed project Mind Map you can start project managing with the iMindMap Project Management Mode.

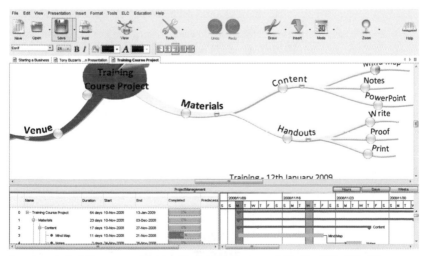

A screenshot of the comprehensive Project Management Mode within iMindMap, showing the Mind Map view, Task Table and Gantt Chart

Mind Mapping for effective project management

You can enter the Project Management Mode by going to the Mode menu and selecting Project Management. You will also now see a Task Table and Gantt Chart in the bottom half of your screen. You can increase and decrease the partition space and select hours, days or weeks in the Gantt Chart. It is worth noting that if a branch is active in your Mind Map this will also be active in the Project Management view, allowing you to connect the two views very easily.

You will see your tasks are structured into Summary Tasks and Tasks. Summary Tasks (main and parent branches in your Mind Map) provide a collective overview of the related tasks within that project area. Detail can now be added to any of your tasks. You have the flexibility to add your task details in two ways: within the Mind Map view or within the Task Table view.

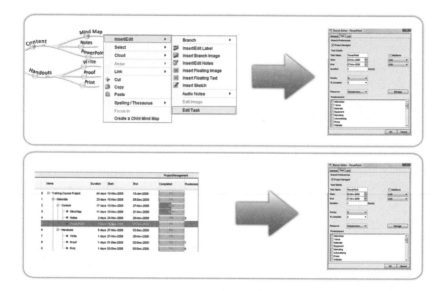

Within iMindMap you can add your task details to your project in the Mind Map view, using the right mouse menu and selecting Insert/Edit > Edit Task. You can also add your task details when you are in the iMindMap's Task Table view, by double-clicking on the task

Here you can start adding in your task details; most of which can be entered on the paper version, but all can be entered into the iMindMap program, which will calculate many of the conclusions for you, saving you more work.

- **Start Date and Start Time** – Specify the date and time when the task should be started (this can be added to a paper version).

- **End Date and End Time** – Specify the date and time when you plan to complete the task. The computer program will automatically display the total duration for the task in the Duration box (this can be added to a paper version).

Mind Mapping for core business skills

- **Duration** – If a start time is added and you know the duration, add this in and the end time will be calculated for you.

- **Milestone** – Select the Milestone checkbox if you would like to set the task as a project milestone. This will disable the End Date and Time drop down list.

- **Priority** – Set the task priority by selecting from 0 to 10, 10 being the highest priority.

- **Percentage Complete** – Enter and update your completion percentage as you progress through the task. This can be reflected in the Task Table view as shown below and via Project Progress icons placed on each of your task branches within your Mind Map.

	Name	Duration	Start	End	Completed	Predecessor
17	Marketing	3 days 24-Nov-2008		27-Nov-2008	0%	
18	● Website	2 days 24-Nov-2008		26-Nov-2008	0%	
19	● Email	1 days 26-Nov-2008		27-Nov-2008	50%	18
20	Adverstising	1 days 01-Dec-2008		02-Dec-2008	0%	
21	● Press	1 days 01-Dec-2008		02-Dec-2008	0%	18
22	Equipment	47 days 27-Nov-2008		13-Jan-2009	0%	
23	Projector	1 days 27-Nov-2008		28-Nov-2008	0%	
24	● Buy	1 days 27-Nov-2008		28-Nov-2008	0%	
25	Laptop	1 days 05-Jan-2009		06-Jan-2009	0%	

You can record and track your project's progress using iMindMap's Percentage Complete function. This data is displayed in Task Table view

In this program, the times and duration of Summary Tasks cannot be edited as they rely on their Tasks to define this information. In addition, you can batch selected tasks and apply the same task settings to save you time, and you can add additional tasks to your project. You can also delete tasks.

Steps 3 and 4: Manage and share

Paper Mind Maps can be shared among colleagues as a hard copy on paper, or can be scanned into the computer and circulated electronically. If you are using the iMindMap program you can simply print off your completed Mind Map, table and Gantt Chart by clicking on Print and selecting what you want to print using the check boxes.

Your team or the organisations you are communicating with do not need to have the iMindMap software installed on their computers in order to receive and view your Mind Map, you can easily export your project to more widely used software, such as Microsoft Project, if you want to add further details or to share information with external clients. Your iMindMap can also integrate with Microsoft Office programs such as Outlook, which means you can export your task data into your Outlook calendar, thereby ensuring that tasks are completed on the correct dates and within the right timeframes. You can even send this information to any of your tasks' allocated resources if they are in your Outlook Address Book. In this way you can keep your whole team up to date and on track.

Once you have set up your project within iMindMap you can use the Project Management Mode to manage it too. The Gantt Chart provides an ideal timeline for you to follow to ensure that your project stays on track – you can amend the view to display days or weeks for more detailed management.

You can update your task's progress using the Percentage Complete facility within the Task Editor. This data will then be added to your Mind Map in a pie chart format, which will then give you a quick indication of how the project is developing. The system is also completely flexible, allowing to you update, add or amend any tasks or task information as your project progresses.

The most daunting project

The 9/11 terrorist attack of 2001 not only destroyed New York's Twin Towers, it also demolished an electrical substation for lower Manhattan located at 7 World Trade Center. This shut down the electrical supply for most of Manhattan south of 14th Street, including Wall Street. Con Edison, the major utility for New York City, provides electricity, gas and steam services to more than 3 million customers. Immediately after the attack, Con Edison's chairman sent a simple order to all company forces to 'Get the lights back on'.

Con Edison used mind-mapping software of the day (before iMindMap) to develop their action plan and to manage the enormous volume of data and documentation this cataclysmic event generated. Real-time data was displayed on a large, high-definition plasma monitor to facilitate accurate decision-making, updating and follow-through. The Mind Mapping and strategic planning were led by Al Homyk, Director of Compliance.

The 'mega' Mind Map that was created included eight branches (see page 130), which addressed the following issues:

1 **Sampling** – What samples were required, where they were taken, and the data that resulted from these.

2 **Environment, Health and Safety (EHS) inventory control** – What protective clothing and respiratory equipment was required and the logistics of getting it to the workers.

3 **Communications** – Memoranda and letters informing workers on work area hazards and procedures.

4 **EHS support** – Detailed 24/7 manpower coverage schedules.

5 **Safety** – Inspection tours to enforce procedural adherence.

6 **Accounting** – Tracking spending and ensuring vendor availability.

7 **Electrical generators** – Over 100 temporary electrical generators were installed and connected to a temporary street grid to repower lower Manhattan.

8 **Regulatory notifications** – Temporary waivers for asbestos work notifications and work-hour limits were sought and granted in accordance with regulations.

Mind Map branches were hyperlinked to spreadsheets and documents containing hundreds of pages of data. The Mind Map became a roadmap for quickly finding detailed information and managing the overall EHS response effort.

A sense of fear was widespread in the early days after the 9/11 attack. A normal reaction to fear in many people is for the emotional side of the brain to become 'hijacked', which interferes with rational thinking. The mind-mapping technique helped workers to unlock themselves and focus on the positive action of how they could best respond to this unprecedented event.

The original 9/11 Con Edison Mind Map

After the 9/11 destruction of the New York City World Trade Center, Lisa Frigand, a project specialist in economic development for the city's utility company Con Edison, was closely involved with the rebuilding of downtown Manhattan. Her efforts often revealed difficulties caused by the web of individuals, groups and organisations involved. This could have been overwhelming, but fortunately she knew mind-mapping specialist David Hill, also of Con Edison, who had already introduced her to the technique. Frigand and Hill worked together gathering information from hundreds of sources, including reports, brochures, magazines and the internet, to create a poster-sized 'Proto-Mind Map' of all the parties involved in the restoration of lower Manhattan. The main branches they created were government, civic, infrastructure, properties, victims and memorials. They also identified what was created after 9/11.

When the Proto-Mind Map was completed it showed everyone involved and their connections in a brain-friendly manner (see page 131). People involved with the rebuilding effort were able to see not only the big picture, but also the detail of this enormous effort.

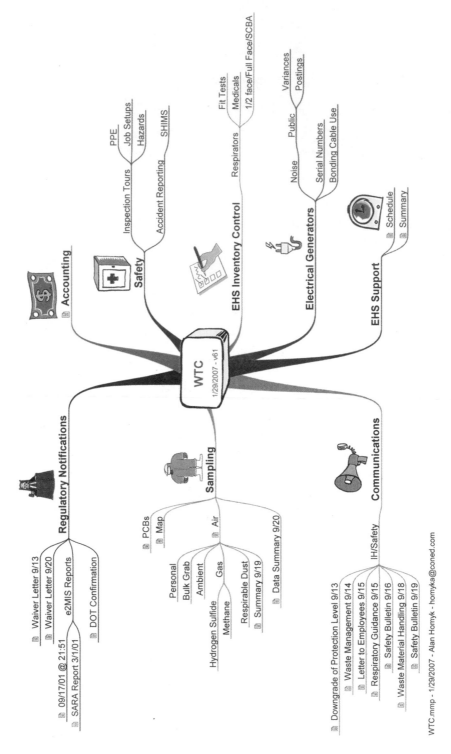

A computer-generated *Mind Map* showing how Al Homyk managed the rebooting of power post 9/11 in New York

WTC.mmp - 1/29/2007 - Alan Homyk - homyka@coned.com

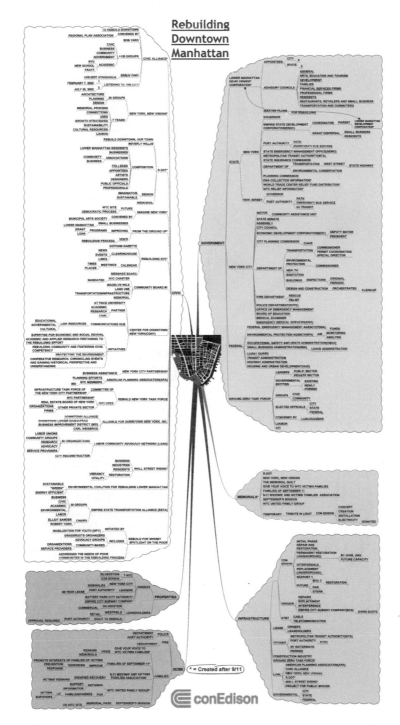

World Trade Center 'Proto-Mind Map' by Al Homyk
© Con Edison

CC conEdison

Leabharlanna Poibli Chathair Bhaile Átha Cliath
Dublin City Public Libraries

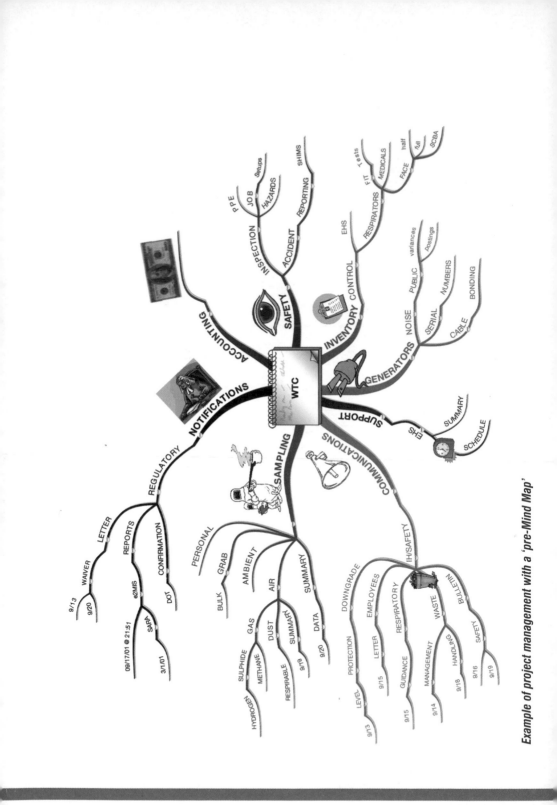

Example of project management with a 'pre-Mind Map'

Planning and managing a project requires an individual or team having the ability to see the end result and work through problems and obstacles to reach the end goal. Seeing a project through to completion often requires changes of direction and compromises along the way, and sometimes even radical rethinks. Mind Maps can allow you to see the bigger picture and find your way through the maze when fully immersed in a project, without losing your cool. Keeping a strong focus on the objective is key to success, and in the next chapter we will discuss another key element of good business: leadership.

Mind Maps
For Business
Online

Leonardo Da Vinci stated the 'everything is connected to everything' – use the Mind Map templates for project management at **www.MindMapsForBusiness.com** and experience how the Mind Map manifests this statement. You will also find articles, tutorials, tips and how-to guides to effective project management.

Mind Mapping is **original, interesting and usable**. A Mind Map cuts out all the **guessing and intermediary steps** and goes straight into **creating dopamine (neurotransmitters)** for the brain.

Po Chung, Director, DHL (HK)

Part 3
Mind Mapping for better business thinking

Leadership with Mind Maps

Mind Mapping, more than a methodology, is a philosophy of life which leads you toward an excellent organisational culture.

ALEJANDRO CRISTERNA, President, TecMilenio, Mexico

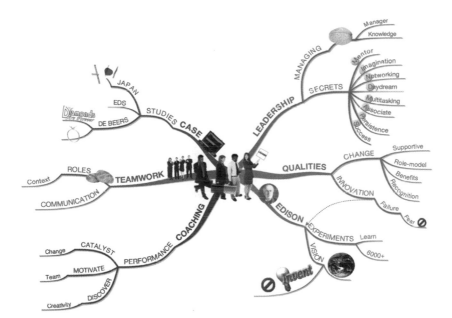

Mind Map summary for Chapter 8

The prime difference between those who become leaders and those who don't is not one of training and application. The difference between the non-realised brain and the realised (genius or leader) brain is focused day-dreaming, and then working to make that dream come true. 'Constructive' daydreaming should be seen as a business opportunity, and the Mind Map as the tool to record it and turn these dreams into golden reality.

Good business leaders know that people are the primary asset of any organisation, and that harnessing the creative and innovative ability of their workforce will help their company break away from the pack and remain competitive in the new global economy. Managing 'the managers of knowledge', that is, the brains in the business, is what leadership is about today. And that means inspiring others to discover their natural creativity, express creative ideas freely, and commit themselves to draw on that creativity indefinitely. Mind Maps are superb visual motivators that can guide the workforce so that they feel valued and part of a team, and build upon the group's own synergy.

Refocusing an organisation with Mind Mapping

To steer his senior management team, Nicky Oppenheimer, Chairman of De Beers, used Mind Maps to capture the essence of the organisation – where it had been and where it was heading. Oppenheimer explains how Mind Maps helped him help his organisation, the world-famous De Beers Company.

De Beers is a strange and unusual company. On the day it was founded over 120 years ago it was the largest and best diamond mining and marketing company in the world. Then in 1930, when Nicky's grandfather became chairman, he set up a structure between De Beers and the Anglo-American Corporation of South Africa to protect both companies from takeover. De Beers came to hold 24 per cent of Anglo while Anglo held 32 per cent of De Beers. The 'crossholding', as it came to be known, certainly achieved its objective, but by the turn of the century this concept was very unpopular with institutional investors and pressure to undo it was becoming heavier and heavier.

In 2001 De Beers was privatised, and as part of the deal the 'crossholding' was undone. The separation of Anglo and De Beers coincided with a strategic review of De Beers which highlighted problems with the company's operating model. This need to change brought a lot of stress into the organisation.

Then, as a final element, Gary Ralfe, De Beers' long-time Managing Director, reached retirement age and was replaced by the current MD, Gareth Penny.

This Mind Map was for a speech to De Beers' senior management to remind them of De Beers' history and to highlight the opportunities ahead.

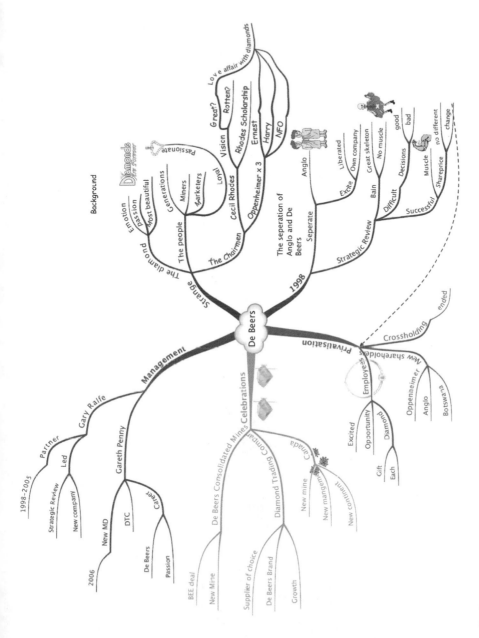

Positioning De Beers

'Eight secrets of leadership exposed' – by Mind Map

This Mind Map was created for the First International Mind Mapping Conference in Singapore where, as was only to be expected, everyone would be talking about and showing off Mind Maps. Jennifer Goddard, co-founder of Mindwerx International Pty Ltd, wanted to honour this objective, but to do so in a different way. What she decided to do was to try to synthesise Tony Buzan's core work on leadership into a simple Mind Map, which she entitled 'Eight secrets of leadership exposed'. Jennifer built her theme around the letters M I N D M A P S, where each letter represented a secret. In presenting her talk she did not show people all the letters right away, but revealed them as she stepped through each of the eight secrets.

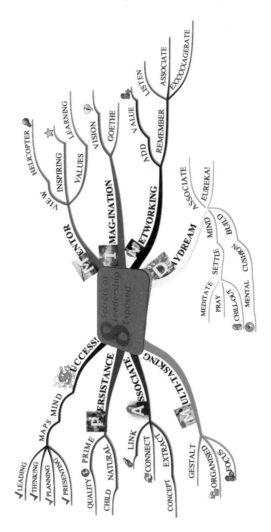

Jennifer was able to bring Mind Maps into her presentation while sharing her own experiences and synthesising the author's key thoughts on leadership. The result was, and continues to be, highly effective. It also neatly enables us to relay to you, in Mind Map form, what leadership should be about.

1 **M – Mentor**: This is about having and being a mentor to provide a helicopter view of things, inspiring one to be a star, and passing on positive values – particularly the value of life-long learning. Jennifer, a master Mind Mapper herself, identified Tony as her mentor.

2 **I – Imagination**: Envision what could be and should be, and always aspire to more. Citing the German polymath Goethe, Jennifer highlighted the concept that when someone commits to something, everything moves to support that commitment. Until someone is committed, there is hesitancy. Whatever you can do or dream you can do, you need to begin to do it. Boldness has genius, power and magic in it.

3 **N – Networking**: This is a true value-adding aspect of leadership, but just networking is not enough. Great networking is about social intelligence and memory. Memory techniques (such as linking a person's name to an object) come into play as you listen, associate or exaggerate people's names or faces to remember them.

4 **D – Daydream**: It is in our quiet times that our minds settle and we find we can meditate or just relax. The aim of this secret of leadership is to build a mental cushion upon which to relax so that the bloom and flow of association starts to work as 'eureka moments' and startling insights hit. Daydreaming is at the heart of creativity.

5 **M – Multi-tasking**: This is about both the specifics and the big picture of the situation. Effective multi-taskers don't just lead from one thing to the next without understanding the big picture and the long-term goals, they organise their thinking and focus on the priorities in an order and way that makes sense.

6 **A – Associate**: We learn and create by making connections, linking things together, and from those we extract new concepts. One key aspect of creativity is the associative nature of thought, which is realised and made real through Mind Maps.

7 **P – Persistence**: This is the prime quality of leadership, without which sustained success is not possible. Very young children demonstrate a natural persistence as they learn, but they lose this as they grow older. However, real leaders maintain this, and, in particular, innovators and entrepreneurs highlight this even more.

8 S – Success: So bringing these together we have M I N D M A P, and the final secret is Success through Mind Maps – how they help us to lead, think, plan and present.

Qualities of great leadership

Human beings can adapt to change but for some it is a reluctant process. The job of a good leader is to spark innovation and establish the conditions where change can flourish and not be feared. These conditions include:

- supportive and developmental working environments;
- visible role models;
- clear and open communication channels (in which Mind Maps can play a pivotal role);
- obvious attractive benefits associated with the change;
- positive recognition for those who are giving change their best shot.

Innovation in the workplace takes many forms but it is basically about converting an idea into an action, with an outcome and tangible result. (Mind Mapping for ideas generation and innovation is covered in Chapter 9.) This could be in the introduction of a new product, a new service, a new business model, a new initiative or a new programme.

Fear of failure and a 'blame culture' are the primary culprits that stifle innovation in businesses today; great leaders need to cultivate an atmosphere where failure and risk are accepted and not derided. Innovation nearly always carries some form of failure, from which ultimately success will usually follow.

Managing change

To bring about change in a team situation you have to be able to apply to the team all the things you apply to yourself as an individual. You have to help that group of individuals in its 'supra-individual' state – the group, the team, the company – to achieve its goals.

The process of change in companies often appears more difficult than it is because there are company structures and processes which are obstacles to change along the way. These changes can be s-l-o-w! If this is the case within your own department, why not use Mind Mapping to radiate a wealth of creative ideas for bureaucratic simplification and dynamic change?

Mind Maps are particularly effective for sharing and explaining a 'leadership vision'. So that the vision can be effective, it is essential that you as leader gather together as many other people as possible who are enthusiastic and inspired by the vision and who are willing to devote their time to helping that vision become a reality.

This requires a great deal of trust. This trust has to be tempered with a very clear idea of what the vision is and how to enthuse others in a way that enables them to understand the details of the change, the mechanics of it, and how they can use their own specific knowledge to help manifest the vision. Effective delegation is crucial in bringing about a change that will deliver a positive result.

Electronic Data Systems

Electronic Data Systems (EDS), the information systems conglomerate, makes the teaching of mental literacy among its employees a prime corporate goal. One main feature of this campaign is the development of leadership capabilities. To accomplish this it was essential to establish a complete understanding of what individual project goals were, and to establish the purpose of the leader or 'champion' for each of the many and various projects.

To identify the role of the champion in each project group, the entire group was given a blank Mind Map, which they then filled in as a group. As Jim Messerschmitt and Tony Messina, the directors of the projects and originators of the Mind Maps, said, 'It worked especially well, took a very short period of time, and everyone had a complete understanding of what we were trying to accomplish and what the purpose of their champion leader was.'

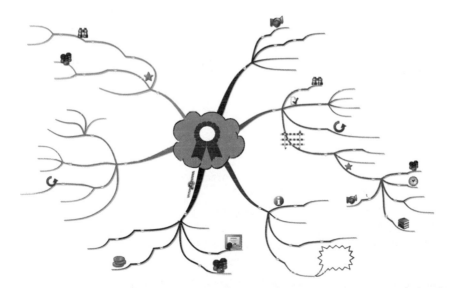

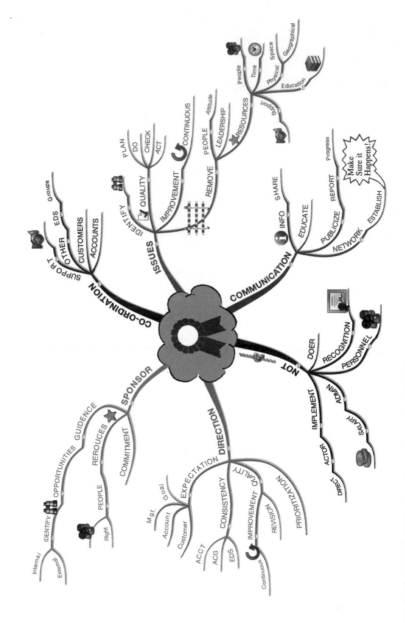

An example of a completed leadership or champion Mind Map

To bring about change in any future organisational endeavour, it is essential to teach each individual 'change manager', i.e. the human brain, to process change management appropriately and then to combine that approach with that of other 'change managers' using the same approach. You can use Mind Maps to consider, refine, select, prioritise and decide on a timescale for this change, then combine individual Mind Maps into a group Mind Map (as explained on page 167) to obtain a collective overview of what needs to be done to put your plans into action.

In all these processes, Mind Maps can help progress the openness and transparency of the vision. In an organisation that knows how to manage change and what change management is, and that knows about Mind Maps, it would be very difficult to find a negative thinker among the 'change makers'.

The Edison approach

More leaders need to take a true 'Edison' approach to innovation. This is not simply achieving a result through trial and error, as this would be an inaccurate description of the innovative method used by Thomas Edison to invent the light bulb. His vision wasn't to invent the light bulb: his giant daydream was to light up the planet at night and so allow all human beings for the remainder of eternity to see whenever they wished throughout the 24 hours of the day (you are probably reading this thanks to his leadership).

Edison was not afraid of failure, since with each experiment (and there were over 6000 of them) he learned a valuable lesson that ultimately moved him closer to his goal – to, literally, enlighten the world. Workplace leaders and managers need plenty of options and have to think quickly, clearly, and in pace with business development and technology; any tools which allow them to do this and to see clearly should be applied: the Mind Map is one such tool.

Coaching with Mind Maps

Great leaders should inspire their staff to discover their natural creativity, express creative ideas freely, and motivate themselves to draw on that creativity indefinitely. It is their job to guide their workforce so that they feel valued and part of a team, and build upon the group's own synergy. They also need to motivate team members who feel burnt out.

Above all, great leaders are willing to explore new possibilities and be catalysts for productive change. They embrace imagination and creativity and they promote innovation within their company. Using Mind Maps opens up the possibilities for constructive daydreaming and positive change.

To encourage supportive working environments with clear and open communication channels, leaders will be only too aware of how crucial it is to coach their team to be more productive and inspire them in a positive way. The problem with terms like appraisal, 360° feedback or balanced scorecard is their negative bias – 'This is what I think of you'. Performance coaching is a very non-confrontational way of discussing strengths and weaknesses and development needs, and Mind Maps are a superb tool to use in this process.

So, let's use an example to demonstrate how Mind Maps can help performance coaching. Two parties, we'll call them Richard and Betty, each create a Mind Map highlighting reds for 'weakness' and greens for 'positive things'. (Amber, for 'development needs', comes a little bit later.)

Before the coaching session, Richard, the leader, creates a Mind Map about Betty from his perspective (see page 147); it shows what Richard thinks that Betty has done well (greens) and not so well (reds), and what areas Betty needs to develop (amber), which come from the reds. Betty also does her own Mind Map independently (see page 148). It's very important that neither party sees the other's Mind Map before the meeting. If Betty sends Richard her Mind Map before the meeting it instantly changes the way that both parties think; it makes Richard hook onto something that Betty has highlighted, or vice versa, so their thoughts are not fully independent.

Richard and Betty have their session and look at each other's Mind Maps. The notion of 'the map is not the territory' comes into play here – so what Richard thinks Betty does well, or could do better, is quite often not exactly what Betty sees. For instance, the biggest positive (green) that Richard sees in Betty invariably is not on Betty's own Mind Map. Richard might view it as an incredible strength of Betty, but Betty may not know that Richard sees it like that, or at all.

Betty is very balanced when bringing her own strengths and weaknesses to the table; she puts in a lot of reds about herself because she wants to show Richard she realises where her weaknesses are. She doesn't particularly want Richard to bring something up that she hasn't thought of. So the process is non-confrontational because in effect they are agreeing with each other about the weaknesses.

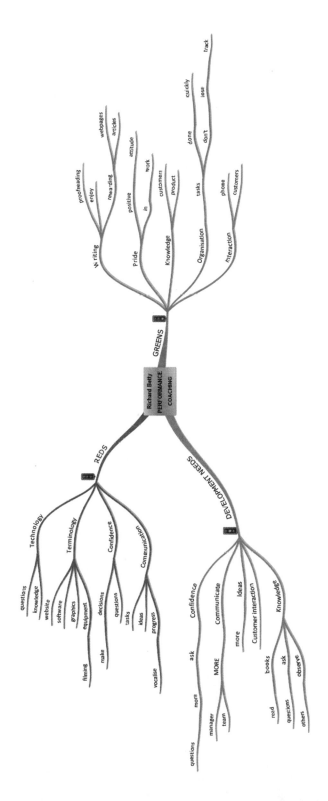

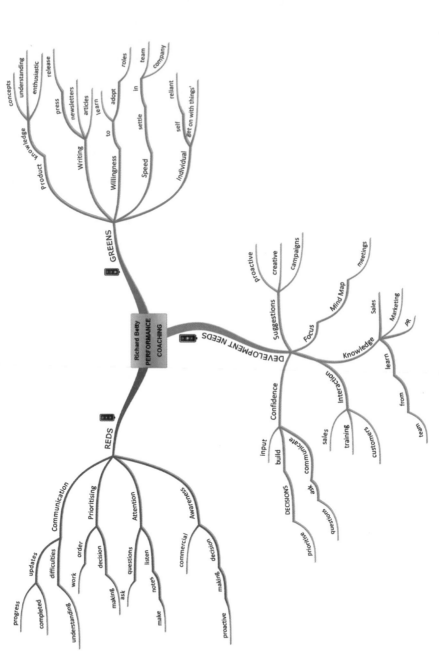

Mind Maps created first by the line manager (page 147) and second by the team member (page 148). The Mind Maps are not the same, showing that each one of us perceives the world differently. To manage and lead other people successfully, we cannot assume we all see the world in the same way. Mind Maps are a quick and easy way to gain insight into someone else's 'reality'

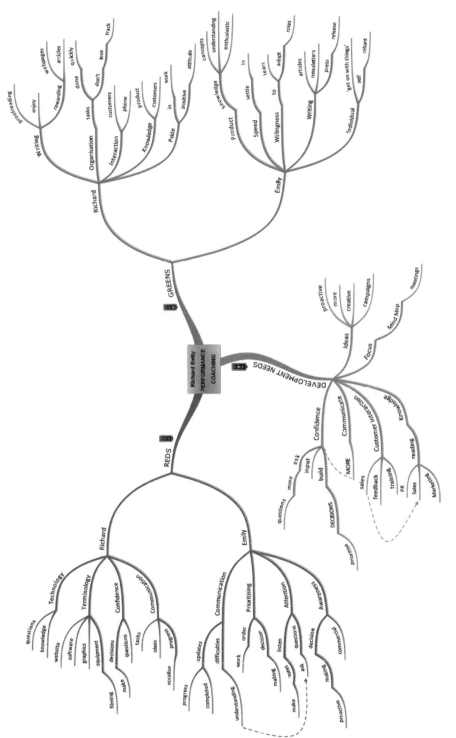

The final Mind Map, which the line manager and team member came together to work on, provides the roadmap forward, focusing mainly on development needs

From the two Mind Maps Richard and Betty create a single Mind Map (see page 149) – not unlike the action of two acetates sliding over each other – adding all reds and greens. As they do this they spend time agreeing as a pair on development needs. This Mind Map technique becomes highly qualitative not quantitative.

From this scenario Richard and Betty keep the green branches green and turn the red branches into amber. The process boils down to Richard asking Betty, 'Where do you think you need help to improve?', while also saying, 'I would like to see you improve in these areas'. Often the areas highlighted on the Mind Map are exactly the same.

Joint Mind Maps lead to consensus rather than confrontation. They avoid the negative scoring systems or spreadsheet 'tick boxes' which are self-limiting. They give no 'weight' to whether Richard gives Betty a 2.5 or 3 out of 5. The leader is never put into the position of having to weigh up demotivating scores.

Mind Maps to inspire team work

Team work is the lynchpin of any business, so making sure the team works well together should be a priority.

One of the most common problems in teams is communication, and this issue can often start when team members misunderstand or do not know what the role and function is of the other members. Mind Maps are a good way of ensuring everyone in the team knows what each member does and what they're good at. In one single sweep a Mind Map can show how the team fits together as a whole, and what each individual does. This Mind Map can be referred to over and over – and revised and updated as things change.

The case study opposite illustrates exactly this sort of organisational change in a particularly tricky business scenario.

Mind Mapping applied to organisational change in Japan

Masanori Kanda is known as one of the most influential entrepreneurs in Japan today and was named the top marketer in the November issue of *GQ Japan* (2006). Here is his Mind Map story.

Faced with global crisis, Japanese companies are thrown into a whirlpool of changes. Survival is the name of the game. Those who can make a successful transformation by proactively adapting to changes will be the winners. Building a strategic organisation is a critical part of transformation to ensure business growth. For me that means the need to shift from a traditional pyramid-shaped organisation in Japan into an open and transparent organisation.

I am reorganising my company Almacreations, which I founded in 2007, to leverage on education and consulting expertise. Mind Maps are being used first to draw the existing structure of the company, then to identify where the bottlenecking occurs, and eventually to paint an ideal scenario.

Masanori Kanda, founder of Almacreations

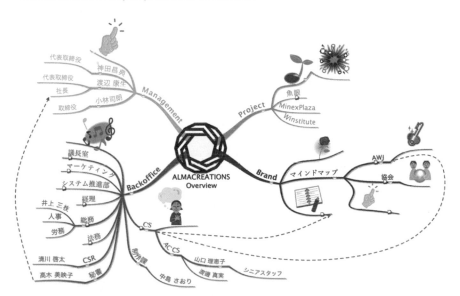

I have produced a Mind Map of each division in the company. Ultimately, through mind Mapping, the entire organisation will be scrutinised from every level of command: top, division, and staff. The individual name for each position is written down on the Mind Map, showing exactly who reports to whom. A Mind Map enables everyone at every level of the organisation to see the status quo, and what is working and what is not. I am involving the staff from the beginning of this process. By doing so, the problems are made visible to everyone. Each must be engaged and committed to co-create a viable structure which is fair and transparent.

Traditional Japanese organisation can be described as having a pyramid-shaped top-down structure. During the high economic growth period in the post-war era in Japan, this type of organisation proved to enhance productivity. Human resources were placed in one of the vertically aligned layers of the hierarchy. Orders came down from the layer immediately above, and when diligently followed by everyone, the organisation functioned efficiently. Each employee was evaluated by their immediate boss, regardless of the ability of the assessor. The relationship was often limited to the assessor and the assessed. There was little or no flexibility of freeing oneself from this closed loop of communication. In such a vertically segregated organisation there was no room for free-flowing communication or information-sharing across functions.

New ideas and values are often generated through communications between and among people from diverse backgrounds and responsibilities. When the barriers between functions and divisions are eliminated, transparency and visualisation of the real issues results. Radiant organisation provides time and space for communication in every possible direction across the organisation, empowering each individual to make a difference.

I conducted a two-day mind-mapping camp with my employees. Everyone was engaged in drawing where each one stood in the organisation at that period. It was an experience of identifying who had been doing what and for whom for the first time.

It was assumed that an 'information network' connected everyone in the company. However, this proved wrong. People who took part in the camp discovered, to their surprise, that they hardly knew what the person sitting next to them was actually doing. In the age of information and communication technology (ICT), beneath the intricate information web individuals are increasingly alienated from each other when sitting in front of a computer. In the past you could overhear the telephone conversation of your neighbour sitting next to you and you could get the sense of what was going on from the way he or she sounded; now, with each person quietly sitting in front of their computer, perhaps with headphones on an MP3 player, you can hardly tell what is going on from their silence. Work is often carried out in quiet, with minimum dialogue between workers. In an isolated environment it has become increasingly difficult to expect people to work together as a team. Everyone seems to be working with an assumption that each is playing a necessary role. But is it true? This is the question I posed with others during the two-day mind-mapping camp.

Eight teams drawing eight Mind Maps

Eight teams representing eight divisions of Almacreations each drew a Mind Map of their division on a large blank sheet of paper. Each team consisted of four to six people. This was an eye-opening experience for many; not only did they find out for the first time what others were doing, they also realised the gap between *what they thought was* and *what actually was* the work of each individual in their division.

A Mind Map of Fish Eye project members, Almacreations

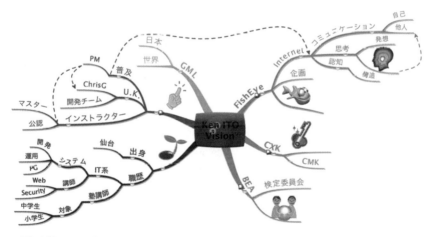

A Mind Map of ITO vision, Almacreations

Then participants were given opportunities to look at the Mind Maps of other teams. They observed what others were doing and were made aware of the importance of communication between and among different divisions. For instance, the marketing division should exchange information and ideas with the system development division to come up with creative ideas and solutions. Synergy can be created through the fusion of ideas. Cross-functional exchange is an extremely important driver of creativity.

The assessment system of individuals was exposed and the bottlenecks were captured on the Mind Maps. The rationale of how each division was organised was to be verified and corrected if necessary.

This can be quite a scary exercise for many, because their raison d'être can be questioned. It is also an opportunity for change and to polish one's abilities to enhance value. There is no need for someone to stand still when faced with a threat.

I plan to use Mind Maps to set objectives through open and free communications in every direction throughout the organisation, and give leadership through objectives, incorporating optimum assessment system. This leads to the next step of identifying the problems of inefficiency and unfairness in the distribution of work, i.e. the job-sharing process. As things become visible and transparent, apparent problems are identified and necessary changes for improvements can be explored. It also becomes possible for each individual to choose the most relevant person for them to report to, instead of having to live with the boss who happens to be above them in ranking. Thus employees are liberated from feeling stuck, which also poses an excellent opportunity for introspection into one's own work and responsibilities. People start to pay more attention to what they are doing and become inspired to work together as a team. I am eager to apply Mind Mapping to step up reorganisation and revitalisation of human capital by freeing up the potential of the mind. iMindMap in particular is useful in making the organisation transparent.

I am planning to build a project-led team using Mind Mapping. Each member of the team will be closely interlinked to multiple functions in the organisation to successfully design and execute the project. Relevant information is to be obtained and exchanged through cross-functional communications. The members of the project team are expected to leave behind their titles in their division and work as a team. This project-led organisation can be the strategic organisation that empowers human resources.

Mind Mapping can play a pivotal role in the process of developing a sustainable organisation that is adaptable to rapid changes today. With open and transparent cross-functional communications in all directions, the organisation grows to become more fair, resilient and effective. The enhancement of morale among employees through fair assessment and feedback loops can be expected. Radiant communications in all directions can generate powerful ideas and problem-solving as well as conflict resolution capabilities. Instead of a mental block, this is a fertile nursery for creativity and innovation.

Great leaders inspire great teams; whether to follow him or her and work hard to achieve the ultimate goals of the business, or simply to show loyalty to the company and its ethos. Working with your colleagues and guiding them through use of Mind Maps can also encourage them to realise how important their individual contributions are. Giving them the opportunities to exercise their creativity and to work as a team allows them the freedom to think around the subject and often to come up with some exciting new solutions. The next chapter will demonstrate how important Mind Maps are in the crucial business skill of generating new and innovative ideas.

Mind Maps
For Business
Online

Employee performance management is the key responsibility for all good managers, but often in today's business world, those who are responsible barely have any time in their overflowing agendas. Try using the performance coaching templates provided at www.MindMapsForBusiness.com and see how Mind Mapping can help improve your team. You will also find articles, tutorials, tips and how-to guides relating to leadership.

Mind Mapping for ideas generation and innovation

People often think that to have the vision, to form the idea and to write it up is sufficient. It's not; it's only the beginning. It's like looking across many cliffs, and you have to be able to navigate your way. It can be all nice landscape, it can all look green, but it's not the same – you have to keep 'knowing the way you are going'. Only with constant vision can you do this. The Mind Map is the manifestation of the vision.

SHEIKH HAMAD BIN EBRAHIM AL KHALIFA, Intelnacom

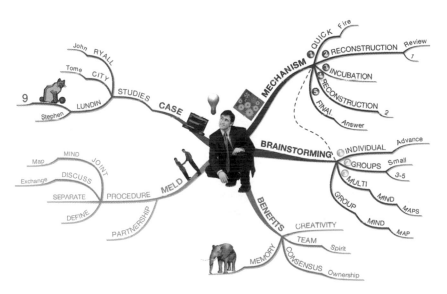

Mind Map summary for Chapter 9

It goes without saying that creativity can – and should – be applied to all areas of your business. It is also recognised that being creative can be difficult when you are obliged to work within codes of conduct and rules and regulations which seem to deaden all levels of thinking. That is precisely when you need to look for fresh perspectives through the use of Mind Maps. This may take you or your colleagues out of the 'comfort zone' at first, but it soon becomes exciting and liberating whether you are in meetings, managing clients and projects, or developing a new business strategy.

Accessing your current knowledge base to promote new concepts is critical, and Mind Maps are the thinking tool to do just that and unlock your brainpower. Unlike linear thought processes, Mind Maps reflect the internal Mind Maps of your brain. If you have lost sight of your goals, or the bigger picture has become blurred, draw a Mind Map and the overview that emerges will bring clarity and potential to the forefront. Mind Maps are based on the fundamental principles of creativity and so they are perfectly suited to supporting ideas generation and innovative thinking. As we have already mentioned, Mind Maps tap into your rational and grounded skills *and* your imaginative and free-associative skills. In addition, the Mind Map is a natural expression of the way your brain works, and has worked, ever since you were a baby.

Dedication and energy are then needed to embed this new way of thinking into the culture of your business. It means really working at it and showing others how to do the same.

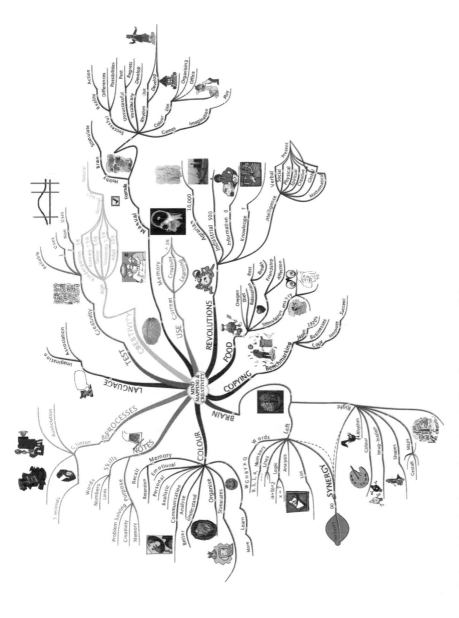

Mind Map made by a delegate at a seminar given by Tony Buzan on creativity

CATS: The nine lives of innovation

Dr Stephen Lundin is a best-selling author, known chiefly for the successful *FISH!* series of books, which has over 7 million copies in print. He is also an educator, film-maker and entrepreneur – and a Mind Mapper. Here is the story of his experience of Mind Maps and creativity.

As a student of creativity and innovation I have long wished that I had something to offer the field that I have loved so much. Then, after the success of *FISH!* and *FISH! Sticks*, two books that brought a simplicity to attitudes to work morale, change and innovation (that are often over-complicated), I had an idea. What if I could organise the world of innovation in a way that simplifies what is often messy and confusing, especially to the analytical and strategic minds that populate our businesses?

For two years I looked for an organising structure. While taking a morning walk a black cat crossed my path. My first thought was 'Bad luck'. Then I said to myself, 'Curiosity killed the cat'. Later that same day I asked an audience to whom I was speaking if anyone there had ever seen a cat die of curiosity. And they said, 'Dogs and cars, yes; curiosity, no'. I wondered about this. Then it struck me. The warning contained in this oft-quoted phrase is telling us to stay in our place: 'Don't rock the boat.'

But there is another old saying: 'Cats have nine lives.' And since my model had nine components I decided on 'The nine lives of innovation' as a title. All of this is just a way to set up what follows. As I wrote the book *CATS: The Nine Lives of Innovation*, I found Mind Mapping popping up in a variety of places. Below are the titles of the nine lives, and after some of the lives I indicate the connection to Mind Mapping.

- **Life 1: CATS create an innovation-friendly environment** – Mind Maps can be used as a portable environment for innovation. The mind-mapping process, with its colours and imaginative shapes, is a greenhouse you can carry with you. The very nature of Mind Mapping creates an innovation-friendly environment.

- **Life 2: CATS are prepared for innovation** – This may be the most prominent use of Mind Maps in innovation. The very best preparation for innovation is to have random access to your knowledge. Mind Mapping is a great way to store knowledge so you can call on it at the moment of innovation.

- **Life 3: CATS know that innovation isn't normal** – Mind Mapping is a paradigm shift as it is a non-linear approach to externalising notes.

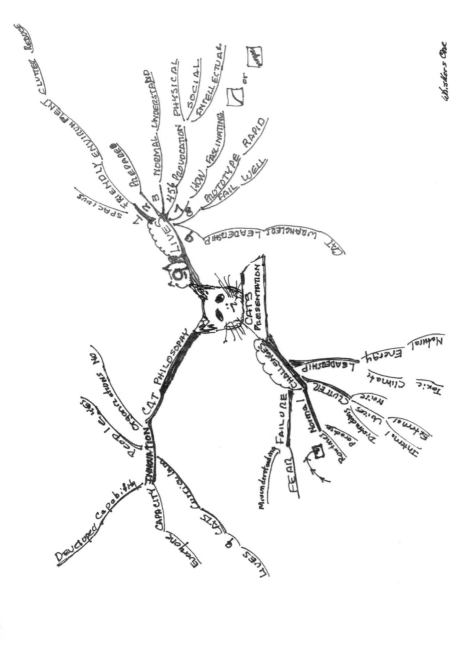

CATS presentation Mind Map

- **Life 4: CATS welcome physical provocation** – Leaving a blank line on a Mind Map is a powerful physical provocation.

- **Life 5: CATS enjoy social provocation**.

- **Life 6: CATS promote intellectual provocation**.

- **Life 7: CATS say 'How fascinating!'** (Tony Buzan is the first person I heard use this phrase.)

- **Life 8: CATS fail early and fail well**.

- **Life 9: CAT wranglers understand natural energy** – A Mind Map is an extreme expression of the brain's natural energy.

By their very nature, Mind Maps automatically utilise all creative thinking skills and at the same time generate ever-increasing mental energy as the Mind Mapper moves towards their goal. The informal nature of Mind Maps also helps to encourage playfulness, humour and innovation, which means the Mind Mapper is not so restricted by formal thoughts and ways of approaching business problems, which allows them to stray far from the norm and as a result produce a truly creative idea.

The Mind Map is simply an image of your visualised concept with associations radiating out from the image on organic branches. These branches include their own images, which radiate and have one keyword per branch. By allowing the Mind Mapper to view a great many elements at once, Mind Maps increase the probability of creative association and integration and enable the brain to track out ideas that normally lie in obscurity on the edge of thinking.

Psychological research has identified several fundamental elements in creative thinking, including the use of colours, shapes, dimensions, unusual elements, the adjustment of conceptual positions and response to emotionally appealing objects – all of which Mind Maps embrace.

The Mind Map as a creative thinking mechanism

If you find you need to brainstorm an issue, deliver a promotional campaign or a marketing idea, make a pitch for a deal or simply discuss a problem within the company that requires a creative solution, creating a Mind Map of the situation is an excellent way of coming up with innovative ways to address the matter.

Here is a simple five-step mind-mapping process for you to follow to create your own brainstorming Mind Map – remember to follow the basic rules of true Mind Mapping as set out in Chapter 2.

1 The quick-fire Mind Map burst

Begin by drawing a stimulating central image that represents the general topic of interest and which encapsulates what it is you want to achieve. Your image should be placed in the centre of a large blank page and from it should radiate every idea that comes into your mind on that subject. For about 20 minutes you should let the ideas flow as quickly as possible.

Having to work at speed unchains your brain from habitual thinking patterns and encourages new ideas. Many of these new ideas may at first seem absurd; however, do not disregard these ideas yet, as often they hold the key to new perspectives and the breaking of old habits. The best solutions come from the germ of an idea, and you want to encourage as many new thoughts and creative ideas as you can at this stage, not stifle them or stop the ideas from coming.

2 First reconstruction and revision

Have a short break, allowing your brain to rest, and then begin to integrate the ideas generated so far. Once you've done this, make a new Mind Map in which you identify the major branches; categorising, building up hierarchies and finding new associations between your preliminary ideas.

It may become noticeable that similar or identical concepts are present in several different places of your Mind Map. These should not be dismissed as unnecessary repetitions: they are fundamentally 'different' in that they are attached to different branches. These peripheral repetitions reflect the underlying importance of ideas which are buried deep within your store of knowledge but which actually influence every aspect of your thinking.

Following your brain's flow, the Mind Map explores your current thought in this new centre to replace the old. In due course this new centre will itself be replaced by a new and even more advanced concept. The Mind Map therefore aids and reflects intellectual exploration and growth.

3 Incubation

After completing the above steps, take a break – sudden creative realisations often come when the brain is relaxed, such as when sleeping, daydreaming or running. This is because such states of mind allow the Radiant Thinking process to spread to the farthest reaches of the brain, increasing the probability of mental breakthroughs. The potential of focused daydreaming to help generate ideas should not be underestimated. Albert Einstein did it to help him visualise and arrive at his famous theory.

4 Second reconstruction and revision

After incubation your brain will have a fresh perception on your first and second Mind Maps, so it will be useful to do another quick-fire Mind Map burst. During this reconstruction stage you will need to consider all the information gathered and integrated in stages 1, 2 and 3 in order to make a comprehensive final Mind Map on a fresh sheet of paper.

5 The final stage

Using your final Mind Map, you now need to search for the solution, decision or realisation to your original creative problem. This often involves doing further work on your Mind Map – making connections between branches and perhaps adding further sub-branches. The answer may not present itself straight away, so be patient, take another incubation break if you need to.

Business brainstorming

The Mind Map is by definition a trigger device for your brain. To realise the brain's full potential all you have to do is use it as it was designed to be used. This again needs to be put in the context of the poverty of traditional brainstorming methodologies – which are linear, list-based and word-based. It is not what your brain needs. Such approaches are anti-creativity; every idea put down is immediately isolated from all the other ideas – it's like entering your brain with a pair of scissors and snipping all the connections between your multi-million brain cells.

Using Mind Maps will help you overcome problems with brainstorming, such as mental blocks or paucity of ideas. Instead of metaphorically standing under Niagara Falls with a teacup worrying that you won't get any water, you will literally 'free flow' and cascade with unlimited creative ideas.

And yet the Mind Map, even though it gives you a free rein, also creates a thinking structure and gives you focused options as your groups create the overall version.

The simple 'two-step' Mind Map brainstorming formula is:

1 Put an image in the middle of the Mind Map to represent what you are brainstorming.

2 Allow your brain to associate and imagine and radiate out everything associated with your central image and idea.

How not to brainstorm ideas

Have you been in this scenario? You are part of a group of people coming together to discuss a new direction, new business opportunity or new product development. In the roomful of people you are with, everyone is expected to throw out ideas to be written onto a flipchart. However, as soon as people start shouting out responses, the brainstorming session grinds to a halt, because as soon as someone shouts out something, other people will try to build on that idea.

It is a standard human brainwave pattern, just like note-making or note-taking from the bottom of one line to the next. You have your own creative ideas but you'll look at what other people are doing and it will start to influence your thinking. You are no longer brainstorming, you are reacting to what somebody said. And that often results in a scenario of a small group dominated by more forceful personalities communicating their ideas – which is not really a group brainstorming session at all and will come up with only a few innovative ideas.

Brainstorming with Mind Maps

Brainstorming doesn't have to take place in a group environment to generate new and innovative ideas. As discussed above, sometimes working this way can actually stifle creativity. Instead, try getting people to prepare for a group session by brainstorming and working individually with their own Mind Map first so that they can come to a meeting with more ideas already sketched out. Define the subject clearly and concisely, set the objectives, give the members of the group all the information that might be relevant to their deliberations and let them go away and think about it individually. Ask each member of the group to spend at least one hour doing a quick-fire Mind Map burst and a reconstruction and revision Mind Map that show major branches.

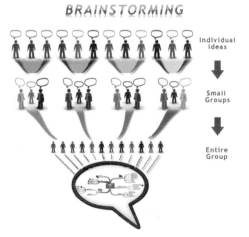

Mind Map of brainstorming with groups

Once the individuals concerned have come up with some of their own ideas, get everyone together and ask them to work in small groups of three to five. In each group allow the members one hour to exchange their ideas and add to their own Mind Maps the ideas generated by other members; your thinking will not be as influenced to the same extent as in standard scenarios because you've already generated your own Mind Map.

Everyone can see everyone else's Mind Maps, and it is essential that a totally positive and accepting attitude be maintained so that even the strongest communicator cannot simply bulldoze through and dominate. Whatever idea is mentioned by an individual should be supported and taken on board by all the other members. In this way the brain that has generated the idea will be encouraged to continue exploring that chain of association. The next link in the chain may well turn out to be a profound insight, emanating from an idea that might have originally seemed weak, stupid or irrelevant.

Multi-mind Mind Maps

Having completed the small group discussion with mini Mind Maps, the group is ready to create its first multiple-mind Mind Map. This can be done by the whole group, one good Mind Mapper from each small group, or by one individual who acts as scribe for the whole group using a large screen or A0-sized sheet of paper. Colour and form codes should be agreed in order to ensure clarity of thought and focus. Basic Ordering Ideas should be selected for the main branches, and all ideas should be incorporated in the Mind Map, the group still maintaining its totally accepting attitude. This technique enables you to unite with a shared vision, because everyone in the room realises they have created the Mind Map together and no one has exerted excessive influence on other people's thinking from the outset.

As in individually creative Mind Mapping, it is essential to let the group Mind Map 'sink in'. Once again the mind-mapping brainstorm process differs markedly from traditional methods, in which the pursuit of ideas tends to be non-stop verbal and analytical activity until a result is achieved. Such approaches use only a fraction of the brain's capabilities, and in so doing produce a result which is less than this fraction. In other words, by eliminating so many of the brain's natural thinking skills, the synergetic relationship they have with the few skills that are used is also lost.

After incubation the group needs to do individual quick-fire Mind Map bursts to produce reconstructed Mind Maps showing main branches, exchange ideas, modify the Mind Maps in small groups, and finally create a second group Mind Map. The two group Mind Maps can then be compared, in preparation for the final stage, when the group will make critical decisions, set objectives, devise plans and edit ideas to produce a final-action Mind Map.

If you prefer, the final Mind Map can then be created on a computer (the previous versions having been hand-drawn for spontaneity and short sessions) to be shared by the group.

Beyond brainstorming – the group Mind Map

Brainstorming ideas is just one way in which Mind Mapping offers exciting possibilities for groups of individuals to combine and multiply their personal creative abilities. Mind Maps are also hugely effective in encouraging joint creativity in other business areas, such as aiding combined recall, and can assist group problem-solving and analysis, decision-making, group project management and training and education (as discussed in more detail in other chapters in this book).

Within groups, the Mind Map becomes the external reflection, the 'hard copy', of the emerging group consensus, and subsequently becomes a group record or memory. Throughout this process your individual brains combine their energy to create a separate 'group brain'. At the same time the Mind Map reflects the evolution of this multiple self and records the conversation within it. At its best, it is impossible to distinguish the group Mind Map from one produced by a single great thinker.

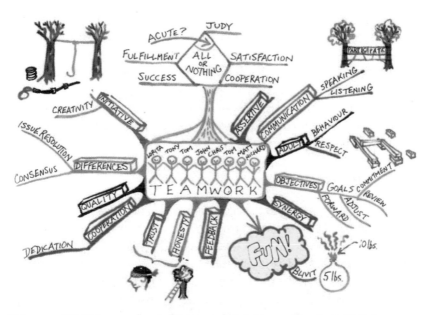

This group Mind Map was created by a team of eight executives from Digital Equipment Corp (now part of Hewlett-Packard) focusing on the development of teamwork. Their conclusions were entirely positive

Numerous studies support the notion that noting your own knowledge and questions in Mind Map form will lead to far better comprehension of the material you read. In addition, working with others will result in the unique perspectives and associations of each individual contributing to a greater overall Mind Map, and a much more comprehensive and integrated learning. We have seen this process already at work in brainstorming.

Tome City: Group Mind Mapping to enhance creativity and imagination

In 2005 nine towns in the Miyagi Prefecture of Japan were merged to create one municipality, run by a new 'Tome City Office'. Each of the former nine municipalities had been run on accepted practices based on their individual organisational manual. Because each manual for the original towns was different, no unified system existed for the new Tome City. The new city organisation started as a very fragmented office without control. Not only were the staff from different town offices with different working practices and styles based on different working manuals, but their numbers had been dramatically cut because of restructuring and fixed-age retirement. The remaining employees were forced to do many more jobs with fewer resources.

In order to improve the new city's systems, the new city's mayor, and leader of the project, decided to introduce Mind Maps. Already familiar with them, he saw the mindmapping exercises as a process to enhance creativity, imagination, communication and cooperation, and to promote proactive and self-motivated employees who would not need to rely on an 'operations manual'.

Enter the Mind Maps

Municipal staff were co-opted for training to discuss the topic 'What is the ideal Tome City?' They were naturally guarded at the start, but their expressions gradually softened and they ended up becoming extremely lively, discussing and mind mapping their vision. As a result of this single training session, it was possible to share and 'visualise' in a Mind Map the respective opinions and values of the people who came from the nine towns. Consequently, the staff members' understanding of each other also became more profound and the primary goal, 'the unification of intention', and the first stage of the objective, was achieved.

In addition, the manager of the city's Personnel Development Department firmly believes in the ability of these Mind Maps to draw out creativity and therefore intends to conduct training continually with the aim of nurturing 'independent, action-oriented personnel'.

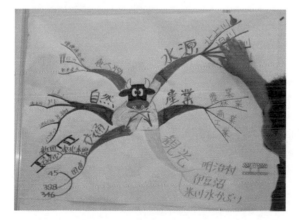

Group Mind Mapping

Benefits of group Mind Mapping

If handled correctly and all individuals are given the opportunity to express their ideas, working as a group to produce a Mind Map can be a very successful process. The group mind-mapping method of thinking and learning is natural to the human brain and is far more enjoyable because throughout the process there is equal and consistent emphasis on both the individual and the group. The more frequently individuals are allowed to explore their own mental universes, the more such explorers bring back and contribute to the group, without in any way losing their own contribution. In this way you get all the benefits of employees working together as a team in which job titles and hierarchy are irrelevant. If all the team members are viewed as being on the same level and having equal opportunity to express ideas, it can generate exciting and innovative solutions and suggestions from all corners of the business. The people in the least creative roles might come up with the most creative solutions.

Even in its early stages, group Mind Mapping can generate many more useful and creative ideas than traditional brainstorming methods, and as the process continues the Mind Map benefits from individual contributions and instantaneously feeds back its own strength to the individual members, thus further increasing their ability to contribute to the group Mind Map.

Group Mind Mapping not only benefits creativity, it also works to build a sense of team spirit. Working together in this way creates an emerging consensus which focuses all minds on the group's goals and objectives, and because everyone's views are considered, members increasingly come to feel that they 'own' the final decision.

The group Mind Map acts as hard copy for the group memory. It also guarantees that at the end of the meeting each member of the group has a similar and comprehensive understanding of what has been achieved. (This again differs markedly from traditional approaches in which members of the group usually leave with an assumed understanding that is often later found to differ widely from the opinions of other members.)

Mind Map for a creativity breakthrough

John Ryall works as a training consultant in the area of management development, sales and strategy for Ryall Development Training Ltd, Ireland, for which company he is also a managing director. He has often used Mind Maps with clients, whether working on a particular team issue, developing a strategic plan, or simply looking at how they can develop themselves in a coaching session. With this type of experience one would assume that Mind Mapping is something that he would also use in his own life without the need for a client to be present. Surprisingly, this was not always the case. John takes up the story.

Although I always looked at Mind Mapping as an extremely valuable tool, and one that I would promote to my clients, I did not seem to relate it to my own life, shamefully. Thankfully this all changed last week.

It was Friday evening and I was sitting with one of my colleagues discussing a new product that we are planning to launch onto the market. The product is aimed at struggling small businesses. We had just found out through one of our associates that a potential client would be very interested in promoting this product to its member companies. We would have to present the 'package' to them in a matter of days, but our associate was confident that if we presented it correctly we would be successful.

So on this Friday evening we were mulling over how we should pitch this product, and how we would approach the government enterprise boards: for support or as a vehicle to promote the product? We were also thinking about how to document what the product is and how it will benefit the client, and how much time we would need to spend with each client to ensure they got what they needed from it.

The more we discussed it, the more convoluted the process got, and the more confused we became. It was now getting late and we had both had a busy week and were tired and losing focus. As we sat looking at the blank sheet of paper on which we had planned to 'document' our ideas, the blankness of the paper reflected the blankness of our creativity . . . it just was not happening.

We knew what we wanted to say, but we could not get it out in a clear, concise and coordinated way. Silence descended to allow us to think for a minute and, almost like someone switching on a light, we both simultaneously said 'let's just mind map it'. We began to laugh as we both realised how idiotic this situation was, given we both worked with clients where Mind Mapping is a natural tool of the trade (but somehow we saw ourselves as separate to that process in some way).

In any case I drew a central image that represented the Strategy Development Product. I simply used a 3-D arrow pointing upwards and from this, our first branch, we put Management Team.

Once we wrote this the juices of creativity and inspiration just flowed. Branch after branch appeared on the page, sub-branches grew from these, and we added the odd picture for aesthetics and to boost association. As we worked on we began to feel less pressure and our energy levels came back; before we knew it we had an entire A4 page crammed with ideas and we needed more paper. The initial presentation document was prepared in another half hour – something which an hour earlier had seemed very far away and had promised to be a very frustrating and tedious process.

I think that Friday gave us an invaluable insight into Mind Mapping. Mind Maps will now be part of every aspect of our lives – both personal and professional. The saying that the carpenter's chair is always broken is very true and we were examples of that. It's time these carpenters fixed their chair.

The two-way Mind Map 'meld'

The two-way Mind Map 'meld' is the most basic form of demonstrating a group mind through a single Mind Map. In this situation the Mind Map is born from the input of two individuals as a partnership on a particular creative project. Just as with Mind Mapping in larger groups, the individuals concerned should define their subject, separate to prepare their individual quick-fire Mind Map bursts and basic Mind Maps, meet for discussion and exchange ideas to create their first joint Mind Map. Again, incubation of ideas is important, following which they can create a reconstructed, revised joint Mind Map which can form the basis for analysis and discussion.

In long-term projects, the joint Mind Map merger or meld has several advantages. The Mind Maps can be used as a way of ordering, recording and stimulating conversation in the many meetings that such a project requires (see Chapter 4). They also enable you to conduct the process over a long time, and in numerous sessions, with continuity and momentum.

As a tool for enabling your brain to think radiantly, nothing beats the Mind Map. Its very form and the way it is designed works with your brain, not against it, and because it is a natural, clearer and more efficient way of using your brain, it encourages exceptional creativity and the generation of innovative ideas. However, in business, ideas are not enough – the way in which they are are acted upon is vital if you wish to achieve success. You need a strategy if you want to achieve both short- and long-term goals, so read on to the next chapter and discover how Mind Maps can perfectly combine these elements.

'Imagination is more important than knowledge' said Albert Einstein. Tap in to the articles, tutorials, tips, iMindMap templates and how-to guides relating to ideas generation and innovations at **www.MindMapsForBusiness.com**.

Mind Mapping for strategic thinking

Mind Mapping has proved to be an invaluable tool for our company, Right Selection, Dubai, UAE. It is a simple technique, having far-reaching benefits the more we implement it because strategy without implementation is no strategy at all.

RAM GANGLANI, Chairman, and GAUTAM GANGLANI, Managing Director of Right Selection LLC Group

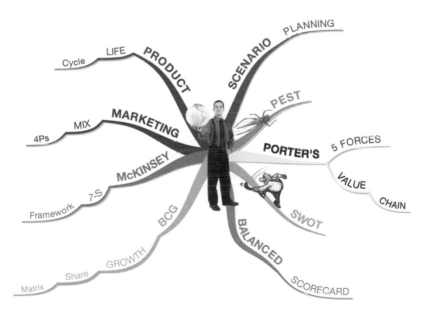

Mind Map Summary for Chapter 10

In business, 'strategic thinking' almost always refers to 'big-picture' thinking. The term describes the way in which people in an organisation think about, assess, view and create the future direction for the entire organisation. It focuses on understanding the fundamental drivers of a business, and on finding and developing unique opportunities to create value. It is the main input to strategic planning and takes into account several aspects such as competences, products, environment and industry, markets, customers and competitors.

Mind Mapping is the ideal facilitator for strategic thinking as there is no better way to assemble, classify, refine, display and share strategic-level ideas and information. The flexible and encompassing nature of Mind Maps supports and adds value to the use of popular strategic-thinking business tools and techniques – from straightforward SWOT analysis to more technical value-chain analysis.

Among the many modern-day strategic thinking and decision-making processes, there are ten key contenders:

1 Scenario planning.

2 Political, economic, social and technological (PEST) analysis.

3 Porter's five forces framework (industry analysis).

4 Strengths, weaknesses, opportunities and threats (SWOT) analysis.

5 Balanced scorecard.

6 BCG growth-share matrix (portfolio analysis).

7 Porter's value chain (identifying sources of competitive advantage).

8 McKinsey 7-S framework.

9 The four Ps (marketing mix).

10 Product life cycle.

In this chapter we will discuss these, while also showing how you can create and use Mind Maps to mirror and enhance these processes – and at the same time make them easier to understand and implement. If you use software-generated Mind Maps with tools like iMindMap you can also integrate them seamlessly on your computer as well as present and export them to a variety of formats such as PowerPoint, PDF or graphics files, making the information easy to share among and within groups.

Scenario planning

What is it?

Scenario planning is a popular strategic planning approach which is regularly used in conjunction with other models to ensure that 'true' strategic thinking is undertaken by those planning. It is a technique that develops various plausible views of possible futures for a business, which will enable a company to narrow down its main strategic issues and goals.

How is it used?

Scenario planning is widely used as a strategic management tool to assist the formation of corporate or business strategy. It can also be used for facilitating group or team discussion about a common future at any level. It works by sketching out a small number of scenarios and stories about how the future may unfold, so that you can consider how to respond to issues that might confront your business. It encourages you to exchange knowledge with others and develop a deeper understanding of the issues of central importance to the future of your business. Scenarios also help to link the uncertainties you hold about the future to the decisions you must make today.

How Mind Maps can help

Mind Mapping enables you to visually sketch out these scenarios and then to delve into the issues thoroughly to identify possible future risks or to uncover hidden opportunities. It also helps to produce ideas and strategies to optimise these opportunities and lessen potential risks.

To mind map scenario planning, as ever, start with a theme in the centre of your workspace; this could be very general or concentrated on a specific issue. Then, radiate thick branches out from the centre to explore key changes, scenarios and possible strategies. The following points provide a framework for your main branches, which you can use to generate and organise your ideas and facts in a logical way:

- External forces – Think of several external forces and imagine related changes which might influence your business; for instance, forthcoming shifts in economics, technology, changes in regulations, demographic changes, etc. Scanning the newspaper for key headlines often calls your attention to potential changes that might affect your business. Mind map these changes and prioritise them using numbers or symbols so that you can clearly identify the ones most relevant to your organisation.

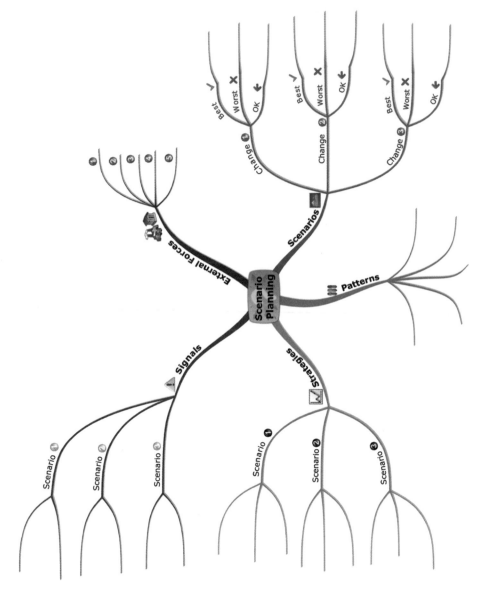

A Mind Map on scenario planning

- **Scenarios** – For each major change you predict, explore three different future impact scenarios (including best case, worst case and OK case) which might arise within your organisation as a result. Highlight the scenarios most likely to affect your organisation.

- **Patterns** – It should now be easy to detect common considerations that must be addressed in order to put you in the best position to respond to possible external changes. Mind map these patterns to isolate them.

- **Strategies** – Suggest what the organisation might do (potential strategies) to respond to each most likely scenario. Highlight or outline the most reasonable strategies you can undertake for each scenario.

- **Signals** – Identify the early warning signals, i.e. the things that are indicative of the unfolding of each of your most likely scenarios.

PEST (macro-environment analysis)

What is it?

PEST analysis is a model that is used to scan the external macro-environment in which a business operates. It helps you to gain understanding of the various external influences on your business by clearly and concisely organising them into four factors: political, economic, social and technological (PEST). These broad external factors and conditions are usually beyond your control and typically present either threats or opportunities to your operation.

Political	*Economic*
Political structures	Economic growth
Environmental protection legislation	Inflation rates
Taxation policies	Disposable income
Foreign trade regulations	Government spending
Consumer protection laws	Unemployment
Competition regulation	Taxation
Employment laws	Interest rates
Pressure groups	Business cycle stage
Political stability	Energy costs
Safety regulations	Exchange rates
	Consumer confidence

Social	Technological
Income distribution	Government R&D expenditure
Demographics	Industrial R&D expenditure
Population growth	New inventions
Lifestyle trends	Technology transfer (speed and direction)
Family structures	Product life cycles
Labour or social mobility	Automation
Educational levels	Production technology
Attitudes and values	The (changing) costs of technology
Consumerism	Technological obsolescence
Health consciousness	Impact of information technology,
Living conditions	internet and mobile technology

How is it used?

As an essential audit tool, PEST analysis can help you forecast key trends and developments in the environment that may impact your organisation. The results of a PEST analysis can then be fed into the strategic planning process to help you determine future business direction and ensure that your company performance is aligned to the most powerful environmental forces. You can also broaden the use of PEST analysis to include marketing planning, business and product development and research reports.

How can Mind Mapping help?

Completing a PEST analysis is very simple and can be done easily via brain-storming. However, the process can be made much smoother and more constructive using Mind Mapping. No matter how simple or complex your analysis is, Mind Mapping will help to increase your awareness of key trends and developments by giving you an 'at-a-glance' picture of what is occurring in your business environment.

After setting a central theme, simply create main branches to correspond to the key forces of political, economic, social and technological influences. Then use the examples of the PEST factors shown in the table to give you ideas for headings for your sub-branches.

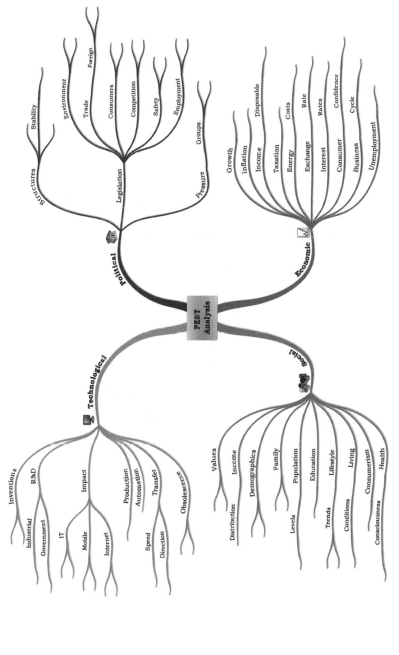

A Mind Map on PEST analysis

Explore each applicable element in depth until you are satisfied that you have covered all angles. Once you have done this, take time to assess which elements will have greatest impact on your organisation and highlight them for emphasis. Also, consider whether any of these elements influence each other directly and show these connections on your Mind Map using relationship arrows.

Porter's five forces framework (industry analysis)

What is it?

The five forces framework, devised by Michael Porter, features five components which can aid in understanding the nature of the driving forces that are shaping the industry your business operates in – including suppliers, buyers, competitive rivalry, new entrants and substitutes. These forces combine to determine the competitive interaction and profitability levels of the relevant industry.

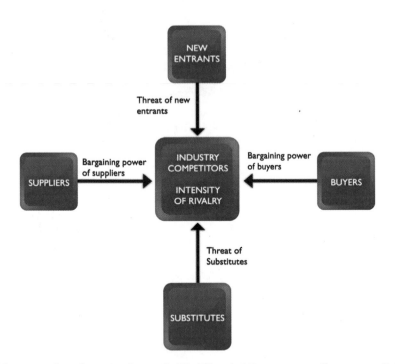

This process has elements of an early Mind Map, but its successor offers a more fluid structure that also serves to stimulate the brain to think beyond the boxes

Source: Reprinted by permission of *Harvard Business Review*. From 'How competitive forces shape strategy' by Porter, M., March/April. Copyright © 1979 by the Harvard Business School Publishing Corporation, all rights reserved

How is it used?

The main purpose of this model is to assist in anticipating opportunities and threats emanating from your competitive environment. This information can then be used to build a strategy to enable you to keep ahead of these key competitive influences and alleviate any competitive pressure you may feel.

How can Mind Mapping help?

A Mind Map presents a more fluid structure for examining the five key forces in your competitive environment than the somewhat linear one shown above. Creating a Mind Map using the five forces as your main branches radiating out from a central theme gives you greater focus for marking out prospective events and evaluating future possibilities.

To form your sub-branches, explore the various elements related to these five forces by using the pointers below.

1 Suppliers

Basic inputs for your product or service are subject to control by suppliers who, depending on their bargaining power, can often dictate pricing and availability. Under this branch, consider how strong your position is against your suppliers of components and raw materials. Are there many or few suppliers in the industry? Are the switching costs from one supplier to another high or low? Is there a possibility of a supplier integrating forward to become a direct competitor? By identifying the best suppliers, you can work with them to create better value and boost your competitive advantage.

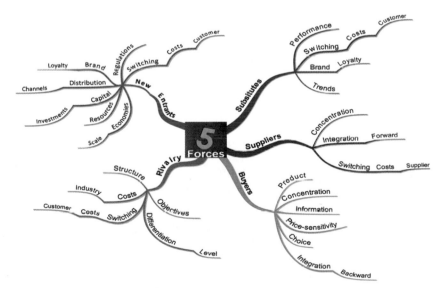

A Mind Map of five forces framework

2 Buyers

Buyers are the people or organisations who create demand in the industry. To determine the relative strength of buyers, you can investigate the following sub-topics and add them to your Mind Map:

- **Product** – A unique product or fad usually lessens the power of customers since they are willing to pay high prices just to obtain the product. On the other hand, where the product is standardised, such as toilet paper, customers will tend to have a lot more influence.

- **Concentration** – If one customer accounts for most of your business, this customer will have a lot of power.

- **Information** – Comparative information that is readily available will tend to empower buyers and give them more influence.

- **Price-sensitivity** – Customers' bargaining power is likely to be high when they are price-sensitive.

- **Choice** – More product choice will increase the power of buyers, who can easily switch providers, whereas few options will limit their influence.

- **Integration** – In the case of business buyers, is there a possibility of backward integration that will make them a direct competitor?

3 Rivalry

This component is concerned with the intensity of rivalry among competitors in your market. The level of competitiveness depends on several factors, which you can use as sub-branches radiating out from this main branch: structure (of competition, e.g. oligopoly, competitive, etc.), industry costs, market growth, differentiation, customer switching costs and objectives (of competitors, e.g. market share growth, profitability, etc.).Competitive rivalry is usually very high for undifferentiated products where customer switching costs are low.

4 New entrants

An industry with low barriers to entry will invariably have intense competition in comparison with an industry with major barriers to entry. Profit margins tend to be higher for an industry with high barriers to entry. Consider the following barriers to entry as your sub-branches to help you ascertain the threat of potential entrants: capital investments, economies of scale, brand loyalty, regulations, customer switching costs, distribution channels, resources.

5 Substitutes

New or emerging substitutes for a product will change competitive forces. Easy substitution reduces demand for a particular class of product as customers switch to the alternatives. Lay out the following sub-branches to determine the impact of substitute products on your industry: brand loyalty, customer switching costs, performance, trends.

SWOT analysis

SWOT analysis

What is it?

A SWOT analysis is by far the most popular strategic planning tool. It provides a clear basis for examining the current situation of a business, project or venture by looking at its strengths, weaknesses, opportunities and threats (SWOT). Strengths and weaknesses are internal to your business and its capabilities; opportunities and threats originate from outside your organisation.

How is it used?

The results of a SWOT analysis are used to formulate plans which capitalise on strengths, minimise weaknesses, exploit emerging opportunities and avoid or reduce the impact of threats. A SWOT analysis can be used as part of a regular strategic review process or in preparation for raising finance, bringing in consultants or making a specific decision. Ideally, a cross-functional team or task force that represents a broad range of departments or perspectives should be involved in carrying out the SWOT analysis. For example, a SWOT team may include an accountant, a salesperson, an executive manager and an engineer.

How can Mind Mapping help?

A Mind Map is a great tool for performing and visualising a SWOT analysis because it can capture lots of information in a compact space and allow you to see connections between contrasting facts and information.

To mind map a SWOT analysis, create a central SWOT theme and radiate main branches to represent the topics: strengths, weaknesses, opportunities and threats. For each main topic, create sub-branches for describing your business's current situation, such as resources, capabilities, reputation, differentiation, customer service, efficiency, competitive advantages, location, quality, business alliances.

Examples of opportunities and threats include business alliances, new products, distribution channels, developing market, new segments, revenue (locating new sources) and regulations.

It is important to note that many of these factors can apply to more than one area of the SWOT, and Mind Maps free you to consider them from different angles and perspectives. Consider which opportunities may also be threats; for example, new market segments could be dominated by competitors, undermining your position. Equally, some threats may become opportunities. For instance, a competitor opening a new market segment for your product or service could mean that your overall market also expands as a result. As well as mapping these out, make use of relationship arrows to emphasise these important connections.

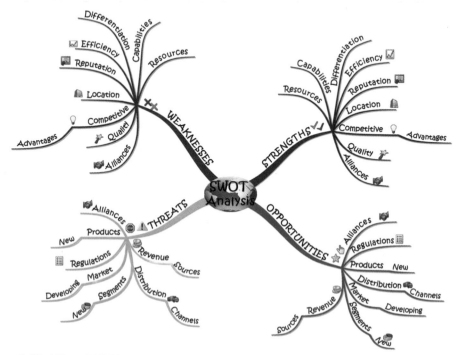

A Mind Map of SWOT analysis

Mind Mapping for better business thinking

Finally, draw attention to particularly important or pressing elements using highlights or strong images.

Balanced scorecard

What is it?

The balanced scorecard is a strategic management concept that enables organisations to clarify their vision and strategy and translate each into action. It encompasses both financial and non-financial measures for a company's objectives so that they can be more effectively steered through all levels of the organisation. By showing how the activities of individual employees link with the strategic objectives of the business, it enables managers to truly execute their strategies and to monitor organisational performance.

How is it used?

The balanced scorecard suggests that we view the organisation and its goals from four perspectives: customer, business process, financial, and learning and growth. Rather than merely collecting feedback using traditional financial measures, it aims to embrace the investment that a company must make in customers, suppliers, employees, processes, technology and innovation in order to be successful in the Information Age. For this reason, a company must develop metrics, collect data and analyse it relative to each of the four perspectives.

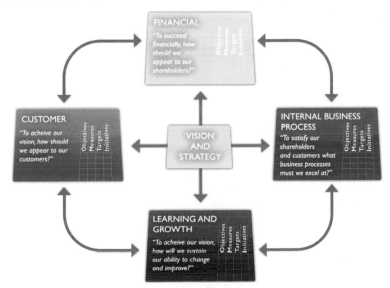

Balanced scorecard

Source: Reprinted by permission of *Harvard Business Review*. From 'Using the balanced scorecard as a strategic management system' by Kaplan, R.S. & Norton, D.P., Jan-Feb, pp. 75–85. Copyright © 1996 by the Harvard Business School Publishing Corporation, all rights reserved

How can mind mapping help?

Designing a balanced scorecard using a Mind Map adds value and discipline to the process of creating measurements by preventing you losing sight of the bigger picture, i.e. the overall vision and strategy. You can transform disparate corporate data into valid information and knowledge easily. In addition, your balanced scorecard can be presented in an attractive and compelling way for more effective communication to others.

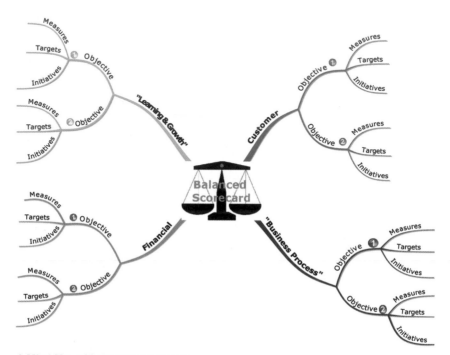

A Mind Map of balanced scorecards

Start by creating a central image and/or topic for your main theme (i.e. your vision and strategy) and then place each of the four perspectives – learning and growth, business process, customer and financial – on separate main branches.

Organise your strategic goals and objectives on sub-branches under the categories that you feel they fall into. Some key questions and considerations could be:

● **Learning and growth** – To achieve your company vision, how will you be able to sustain your ability to change and improve? This encompasses employee training and cultural attitudes related to both individual and organisational self-development. It includes details such as mentors and tutors in your organisation, work systems and ease of communication between workers.

- **Business process** – To satisfy shareholders and customers, what business processes must you excel at? Consider the internal processes that run your business and create its products and services.

- **Customer** – To achieve your vision, how should you present yourself to customers? This element focuses on meeting customer needs and providing customer satisfaction so that they do not defect to other suppliers.

- **Financial** – To succeed financially, how should you appear to shareholders? This includes traditional funding data and other financial related data such as risk assessment and cost benefit analysis.

For each objective, create further sub-branches to devise and report on how you can achieve your goal. Decide on your measures, what methods and metrics you will use to evaluate performance for a specific goal. Also state your targets; what target values will you assign to a particular objective? These will guide managers in focusing their efforts. For example, the areas in which to focus training funds under the learning and growth perspective or the areas you need to improve to create greater customer satisfaction under the consumer perspective. Finally, add in the initiatives needed; list the actions that will be undertaken to implement each objective.

To turn your Mind Map into a more effective communication tool, show the logical cause–effect connections between strategic objectives using relationship arrows. For instance, improving performance in the objectives found in the learning and growth perspective can give the organisation the capability to meet its business process perspective objectives, and so on.

BCG growth-share matrix (portfolio analysis)

What is it?

The Boston Consulting Group (BCG) growth-share matrix is one of the best-known business portfolio planning methods. The business portfolio is the collection of business units that make up your company. Business units can be company divisions, product lines or even individual products – it all depends on how your business is organised and the level of analysis you want to undertake.

The BCG growth-share matrix classifies a company's business units into four categories based on the combinations of two important determinants of profitability – market growth and market share. The four categories – Dogs, Question Marks, Stars and Cash Cows – reflect the different cash demands and cash-generating abilities of the business units in a firm's portfolio.

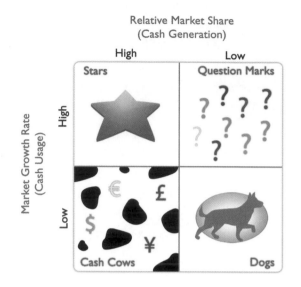

The BCG growth-share matrix
Source: The BCG Portfolio Matrix from the Product Portfolio Matrix, ©1970, The Boston
Consulting Group. Reproduced with permission

How is it used?

The BCG matrix is designed to help a business analyse its current portfolio and
decide which business units should receive more or less investment. As a secondary benefit it also aids in developing growth strategies for adding new
products to exploit attractive opportunities. At the same time it helps to determine when unprofitable or unmanageable business units should be divested.

How can Mind Mapping help?

Although the BCG matrix is a potent tool for viewing a corporation's business portfolio at a glance, its effectiveness can be greatly enhanced when it
is created in Mind Map format. It is much easier and freer to discuss the
resource allocation options between the different business units or products
when you are not visually 'boxed' in by a matrix. Mind Mapping also helps to
overcome some of the limitations of the BCG matrix; rather than assuming
that each business unit is independent, a Mind Map will help you identify
distinctly and display the connections (and non-connections) that usually
exist between business units in different BCG categories.

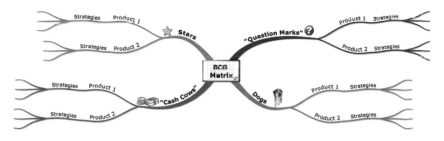

A Mind Map of BCG growth-share matrix

Once you have created a central theme for your portfolio analysis, create four main branches with the headings: Dogs, Question Marks, Stars and Cash Cows. You can use images to represent the four types more powerfully.

From these, you can create sub-branches to name all your divisions or products (business units) that fall into each category.

Dogs have a low market share and a low growth rate and so neither generate nor consume large amounts of cash. Question Marks grow rapidly and consume large amounts of cash, but because they have low market shares they do not generate much cash. Stars generate large amounts of cash because of their strong relative market share, but they also consume large amounts of cash because of their high growth rate. Finally, Cash Cows are leaders in a mature market and generate a relatively stable cash flow that is greater than the cash they consume.

As you delve into an investigation of each business unit, create further sub-branches to convey your strategy ideas, bearing in mind a few features of the unit. Dogs are cash traps because they keep money tied up in a business or product that has little potential to generate cash. Think about divesting such business units. Question Marks must be analysed carefully to establish whether they are worth additional investment to grow market share to become Stars. There is a chance that, if left untouched, they may degenerate into Dogs when market growth declines. If Stars are likely to maintain their large market share, they will become Cash Cows when market growth drops. It is important to weigh up options for maintaining or increasing market share to ensure future cash generation. Cash Cows should be 'milked', i.e. their profits extracted with as little cash invested as possible. These can also provide the cash required to turn Question Marks into market leaders, fund R&D, cover administrative costs of the company, etc.

As each business unit is not necessarily independent of the others, make any connections between units using relationship arrows. This will help you see the overall picture more accurately. For example, a Dog may be helping other business units gain a competitive advantage, and for this reason it may not be a good idea to divest it.

Porter's value chain (identifying sources of competitive advantage)

What is it?

The value chain framework proposed by Michael Porter helps to analyse specific activities through which firms can create value and competitive advantage. Looking at how your organisation creates value is of vital importance because it addresses the economic logic of why your organisation exists in the first place. The more value an organisation creates by offering its customers a level of value that exceeds the costs of its activities, the more profitable it is likely to be. When you provide more value to your customers, you build competitive advantage.

How is it used?

To better understand the activities through which a firm develops competitive advantage and creates value, this framework separates the business system into a series of value-generating activities referred to as the 'value chain'. This series is clearly organised into two categories: 'primary activities' and 'support activities'. The model is well liked by businesses because the way it isolates distinct activities makes it easier to identify opportunities for value creation within each activity. It is also accepted as an effective method for determining how competitive advantage can be obtained by optimising and coordinating the way activities link together.

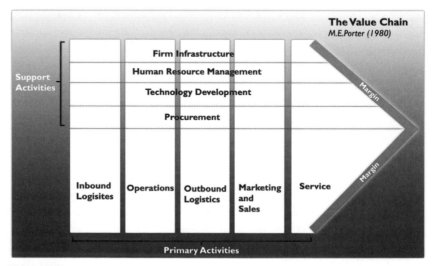

Value chain

Source: Porter, M. (1998) Adapted with the permission of The Free Press, a Division of Simon & Schuster, Inc., from *COMPETITIVE ADVANTAGE: Creating and Sustaining Superior Performance* by Michael E. Porter. Copyright (c) 1985, 1998 by Michael E. Porter. All rights reserved

Mind Mapping for better business thinking

How can Mind Mapping help?

Analysing the value chain using a Mind Map is an extremely effective way of bringing clarity to thought processes on how to create or increase value in each business sequence. You can consolidate facts and information on each main activity all in one place. It also helps you identify clearly the important connections between one area of your business and another. Being able to understand thoroughly the linkages between activities can help you optimise your decision-making, particularly regarding the basis of your competitive advantage (e.g. cost or differentiation advantage).

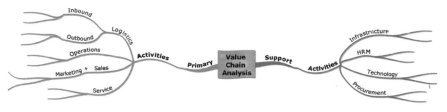

Mind Map of value chain

First, create the central theme of your subject (include an image and/or title) to represent your value chain analysis. Divide your Mind Map into two halves by creating a main branch entitled 'primary activities' on one side and a second main branch called 'support activities' on the other side.

Next format your sub-branches so that you can easily review your current value creation efforts and generate ideas and strategies on how you can maximise value in all areas of your business. Under the 'primary activities' branch, lay out your sub-branches using the following five headings.

- **Inbound logistics** – This is the receiving and storing of raw materials, inventory control, and their transportation to manufacturing as needed.

- **Operations** – The processes of transforming inputs into finished products and services. Operations include machining, packaging, assembly, equipment maintenance and testing.

- **Outbound logistics** – The activities required to get the finished product to the customers. These include warehousing, order fulfilment, transportation, distribution management.

- **Marketing and sales** – The activities associated with identifying customer needs and getting them to purchase the product, including channel selection, advertising, promotion, selling, pricing, retail management, etc.

- **Service** – The activities that support customers after the products and services are sold to them. These include customer support, repair services, installation, training, spare parts management, upgrading.

Under the 'Service' branch, structure your sub-branches using the following titles:

- **Infrastructure** – Encompasses organisational structure such as general management, planning management, finance, accounting, etc., control systems for quality management and company culture.

- **Human resource management (HRM)** – The activities associated with employee recruitment, training, development and compensation.

- **Technology** – Includes technology development to support the value chain activities such as R&D, process automation and design.

- **Procurement** – The purchasing of inputs such as raw materials, supplies, equipment, buildings, etc.

You are now ready to brainstorm ideas and strategies (see also Chapter 9) to decide on a competitive advantage for each of your key activities. The main ways to reconfigure your value chain to create value are by providing lower cost or better differentiation.

To create cost advantage, consider how you can adjust cost drivers such as economies of scale, degree of vertical integration, capacity utilisation, production processes, linkages among activities, distribution channels and sales approaches.

To create differentiation advantage, think about how you can manipulate factors of uniqueness such as policies, location, scale (e.g. better service as a result of large scale), new process technologies, learning and new distribution channels.

Value chain activities are not isolated from one another; rather, one activity often affects the cost or performance of other ones. Show these impacts by using relationship arrows to connect one activity to another and use symbols or images to represent whether the relationship is positive or negative.

McKinsey 7-S framework

What is it?

Developed by McKinsey & Co, this framework describes the seven areas of an organisation that should be focused upon when executing a strategy. Together, these seven factors determine the way in which a business will operate holistically. The seven areas are strategy, structure, systems, shared values, skills, style and staff.

How is it used?

The 7-S model can be used for several purposes, such as to improve the performance of the company, to examine the likely effects of future changes within a company, to align departments and processes during a merger or acquisition, or to determine how best to implement a proposed strategy.

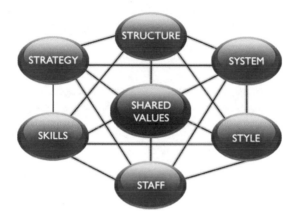

Another example of a pre-Mind Map
Source: The McKinsey 7-S framework. Reproduced with permission from McKinsey & Company

How can Mind Mapping help?

Exploring the 7-S factors using a Mind Map gives you a stronger capacity for understanding your situation so that you can make more effective and coordinated decisions for strategy implementation or organisational adjustments. You are able to capture all your thoughts in relation to each factor much more coherently than if you were writing a list or filling in a table.

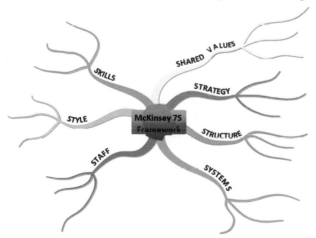

How a true Mind Map can make the interconnections come alive

What's more, you can present your information in a clear, understandable format, which also gives a more professional impression.

The interconnecting central theme of your Mind Map should convey your business's purpose in conducting analysis of the 7-S factors. This will focus your mind-mapping efforts and discussion.

Place each of the 7-S factors (shared values, strategy, structure, systems, skills, style and staff) on main branches radiating out from the central theme. Discuss and explore these 7-S factors, using the following descriptions and considerations to help you:

- **Shared values** – These are the core values of your business that are evidenced in the corporate culture and work ethic. Think about the fundamental values on which the company was built and how strong they are.

- **Strategy** – Define your strategy and your sets of actions designed to reach your identified goals. Also consider how you deal with competitive pressures, changes in consumer demands and environmental issues.

- **Structure** – How is your organisational chart structured – e.g. centralised, functional divisions (top-down), decentralised, matrix, network, holding, etc.? Are the lines of communication and reporting explicit or implicit?

- **Systems** – The main procedures and processes that characterise how the organisation operates: financial systems; hiring; promotion and performance appraisal systems; communications systems and information systems. What are the controls and how are they monitored?

- **Skills** – The distinctive capabilities of your organisation as a whole. What are the strongest skills represented within your company? Are there any skill gaps? How are skills monitored and assessed?

- **Style** – The cultural style of the organisation and how key managers behave in achieving your organisation's goals. Also consider whether employees and team members tend to be competitive or cooperative and how participative the management style is.

- **Staff** – The numbers and types of personnel within your organisation. Are there gaps in required competences and do any positions need to be filled?

Remember that information in one part of your Mind Map may relate to that in another. You can illustrate any cross-linkages from one element to another by drawing relationship arrows. Use symbols or codes to mark up any important patterns that you uncover when looking at your map.

The four Ps (marketing mix)

What is it?

The four Ps are a framework for assessing the four key dimensions of a marketing strategy (also known as the marketing mix). They include:

- **Products** – the products and services offered and their core or peripheral and tangible or intangible attributes.

- **Price** – Pricing decisions for products or services, e.g. penetration, skimming, etc.

- **Place (distribution)** – Getting the product or service to the consumer, e.g. channel selection, direct or indirect, wholesale or retail.

- **Promotion** – The marketing communications decisions designed to generate a customer response or purchase, e.g. advertising, direct marketing, public relations, etc.

How is it used?

The four Ps are parameters that a marketing manager can manipulate, subject to the internal and external constraints of the marketing environment. By using variations of these four components you have the ability to reach multiple consumers within your target market. The goal is to make decisions in each of the four Ps that convey a focused and consistent message to your target market and target consumers to generate a highly positive response.

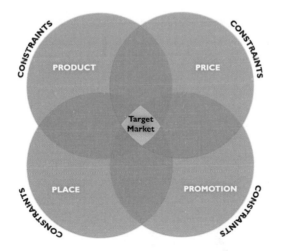

How can Mind Mapping help?

Using a Mind Map to formulate ideas and strategies for the marketing mix increases the chance that you will happen upon a highly successful blend of strategies. Mind mapping enhances the creative process and gives you greater focus, not only encouraging you to be inventive with your marketing approach but also helping you see how marketing elements can be integrated more effectively to better target the consumer.

Create a central theme (image and title) to correspond to your marketing mix and radiate four main branches for each of the four Ps that you are going to evaluate – products, price, place and promotion.

Next branch out further to discuss different ideas and decisions for each area of your marketing mix. Use the following examples to encourage you to think comprehensively and continue to create further associated ideas until your creative energy runs out.

- For Products, think about branding, functionality, design, quality, safety, technology, value, convenience, packaging, repairs and support, warranty, accessories and services.

- For Price, think about your pricing strategy (skimming, penetration, psychological, cost-plus, loss leader, etc.), recommended retail price, volume discounts and wholesale pricing, seasonal pricing, bundling, price flexibility and price discrimination.

- Place includes distribution channels (retail, wholesale, mail order, internet, direct sales, peer to peer, multi-channel), inventory management, warehousing, order processing and transportation.

- Promotion involves promotional strategy (push, pull, etc.), advertising, personal selling and salesforce, direct mailing, leaflets or posters, user trials, endorsements, sales promotions (special offers, free gifts and competitions), public relations, joint ventures and marketing communications budget.

Draw attention to specific ideas or decisions that you find compelling using highlights or strong images. If you find that you have generated a significant number of ideas for each area, try to prioritise them by number so that you can make effective resource allocation decisions among them. Use relationship arrows to link ideas or decisions from different areas of the map that can be integrated into one strategy or plan of action.

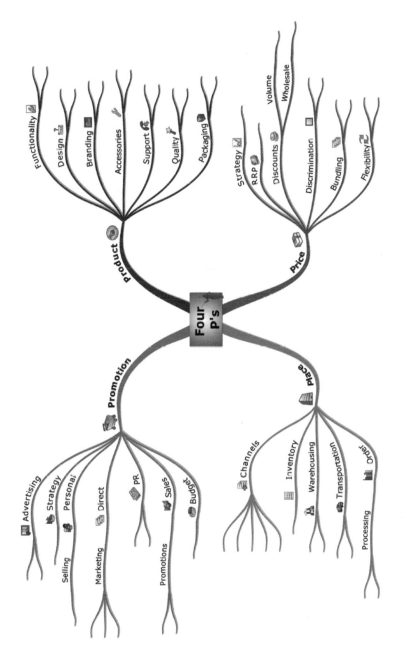

The four Ps

Product life cycle

What is it?

Product life cycle analysis assumes that products go through four main phases during their life cycle: introduction, growth, maturity and decline. These stages are characterised by the revenue generated by the product or product line and their duration can be as short as a few months for a fad item, or a century or more for product categories such as vehicles.

How is it used?

As the product or product line progresses through the sequence of stages, changes will occur in the marketing situation. Businesses typically use the product life cycle to gain insight into the evolving challenges and opportunities that result from each stage. This knowledge can then be used to adjust their marketing strategy and marketing mix accordingly. The primary goals for each stage are typically as follows:

- **Introduction** – To build product awareness and develop a market for the product.

- **Growth** – To build brand preference and increase market share.

- **Maturity** – As growth in sales diminishes and competition increases, the primary aim is to defend market share while maximising profit.

- **Decline** – As sales decline, the firm can opt to maintain the product or product line, harvest it, or discontinue it.

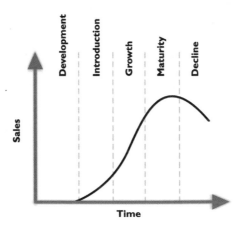

Product life cycle

Mind Mapping for better business thinking

How can Mind Mapping help?

Using a Mind Map for conducting life cycle analysis improves the ability to plan strategically and tactically to respond to the changing conditions in each phase in the life cycle. By visually connecting each element of your marketing mix with each phase of the life cycle, you become more effective in generating ideas to meet emerging opportunities and minimise challenges.

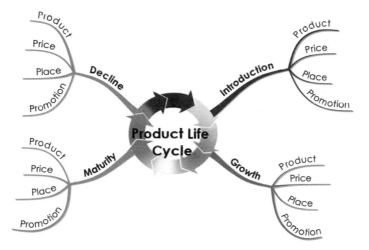

A Mind Map of product life cycle

Starting from your central image or title, create four main branches and label them with the main topics of introduction, growth, maturity and decline. Connect sub-branches from each of your main topics to form the elements of your marketing mix: product, price, place and promotion.

Now it's time to brainstorm your ideas and thoughts for aligning the strategies for each of your products or product lines to meet the opportunities or challenges presented by each stage of the life cycle. The following suggestions may help:

Introduction

For Product, consider branding and quality levels and intellectual property protection; for Price you could perhaps use low penetration pricing to build market share or high skim pricing to recover development costs. In terms of Place it is wise to go for selective distribution until consumers accept the product. With regard to Promotion, think about the best options for building awareness and educating potential customers. Can you offer introductory promotions such as samples or trial sizes?

Growth

For Product, what can you do to maintain or improve quality? What new features, packaging options and support services can be added? The Price can be maintained if you are enjoying increased demand, or reduced to capture additional customers. With regard to Place, what distribution channels can you add as demand increases and customers accept the product? As far as Promotion is concerned, how can you aim your marketing communications at a broader audience? Perhaps you could think about increasing advertising.

Maturity

For Product, what features can be enhanced or modified to differentiate from competitors' products? In terms of Price, do you need to reduce pricing because of new competition? With regard to Place, can you offer incentives to encourage reseller preference over competing products? For Promotion purposes, how can you emphasise product differentiation and build brand loyalty through your marketing communications?

Decline

In terms of Product, can you reduce the number of products in the product line? Think about how to revive surviving products, and think about Price – can you lower pricing to offload an inventory of discontinued products? Can prices be maintained for continued products? With regard to Place you could become more selective with distribution and phase out channels that are no longer profitable. Plan some Promotion – work out how to lower expenditure and aim your marketing communications at reinforcing the brand image for continued products.

Finalise your Mind Map by using highlights to emphasise the strategies that you are most likely to undertake and add thought-provoking images to encapsulate these preferred strategies.

Strategy Mind Mapping in Action   Sheikh Hamad's story

Sheikh Hamad bin Ebrahim Al Khalifa is the visionary behind the creation of Intelnacom, a leading-edge clearing house to commercialise ideas and intellectual property.

As a former Commander-in-Chief and a fighter pilot in the Bahrain Defence Force, Sheikh Hamad was in charge of setting up the Bahrain Air Force. Being also an aeronautical engineer, Sheikh Hamad has set up his own company in aerospace services. He is currently the Chairman of the board of Banagas, a 20-year venture jointly owned by Caltex, ApiCorp and the Kingdom of Bahrain. He was formerly a member of the Supreme Council for Oil and Gas of the Kingdom of Bahrain. He also has private investments in the energy and technology sectors overseas. Sheikh Hamad takes up the story.

In one way, Mind Maps are the notes for brain music. This Mind Map is a planning and strategy outline for a major energy and industrial hub.

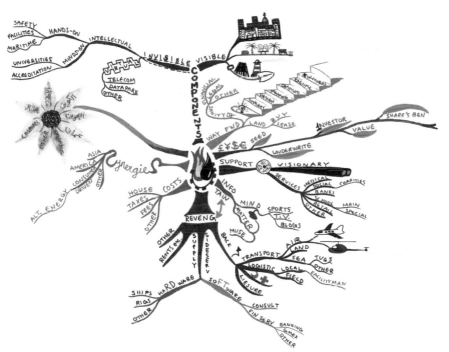

Sheikh Hammad's Mind Map for planning strategy outline for major energy hub

The symbol in the centre of the Mind Map is both a flame and a drop, symbolising the source of energy and the expression of that energy. The flame and the drop are embraced by a symbolised wheel of motion.

This Mind Map blueprint was transformed into a reality, spreading from the Gulf of Arabia and reaching out to China and Africa. The Mind Map can be considered the intellectual seed capital for a multi-billion dollar Solutions Province.

In the components branch there are the Visible, above ground, and the Invisible. On the Visible you have three beautiful images summarising the above-ground elements: one is a city outline with either a palace or mosque in the background; on the second branch the necessary natural elements are symbolised by palm trees; and on the third, a lighthouse, a runway and a spade symbolises the infrastructure.

On the Invisible side, the Datapark houses all elements of data, acquisition, storage, filtration, updating and commercialisation, plus all elements of technology training, curriculums, simulation, safety modelling, and facility management criteria. The Hands-on is the branch that summarises who takes care of everything that involves humans teaching and taking care of other humans. The Minds-on deals with what the human brain can produce for other humans.

The Virtual is the basically unseen kinds of services that one needs, such as telephones, IT connections and the depicting of virtual models. Today in the field of geology you can model virtually the exact seabed of, for example, the Gulf of Mexico. It's like looking at the Rocky Mountains inverted. This is a virtual depiction of something which is not seen with the naked eye. It is therefore a tool that can be used to extract value.

The Way Forward branch is making IT happen, not 'it'! This branch represents a very classical way of moving this kind of massive project forward. You start with the seed, with the concept idea, with an idea, if you like, that starts with the seed idea and seed capital. You begin spending, move on a step, and each step builds on itself as you move towards your goal.

The Money branch shows the money trail from seed capital into the last strata of investors who are happy with 7–13 per cent returns, typically retirement funds and insurance companies. Once you have the original idea in your mind, the money trail starts. The minute you pick up a pencil and a piece of paper, that's already the cost of the pencil and the piece of paper – your first seed capital!

The support engines' main backbone is the Visionary branch. This branch is vital, because for any project, no matter how well you design it, if you don't have vision, you will not know which way you are walking. Without vision, humanity will cease to exist, let alone the economies of projects.

People often think that to have the vision, to form the idea and to write it up is sufficient. It's not; it's only the beginning. It's like looking across many cliffs, and you have to be able to navigate your way. It can be all nice landscape, it can all look green, but it's not the same – you have to keep 'knowing the way you are going'. Only with constant vision can you do this. The Mind Map is the manifestation of the vision.

The Infotainment branch highlights the fact that any venture should have a happy interface between the medium of knowledge and the species. With any project we create in three dimensions, unless we are able to meld this project to allow the dog to walk and the cat to walk, we have failed. We have to make sure we have the right areas for the animals to walk, the right kerbstones for the humans to walk, the right 'aces for the trees and for the birds to fly. Infotainment is in fact informing the human ɛs about our project, while entertaining them at the same time when they visit it.

The Revenue branch, the 'RevEng' branch, outlines the revenue engines, the financial fuel of the project manufacturing (rigs, tankers, and the like) to the other Software branch of banks, exchanges and consultancies. The revenue, of course, is the main artery that feeds the project.

The Supply branch of the main RevEng branch is the branch that offers support outside. God created oil in the most difficult places on earth! It is either under a desert, or a jungle, or a Siberian land waste, or in the Arctic with deep seas and high winds, so you need support services. You need helicopters; you need aeroplanes; you need oil spill or disaster control mechanisms and apparatus. You need diving treatment for diving accidents, and so on.

On the Back-up sub-branch, all support services are noted, from air to sea to medical, plus total environmental disaster control and reaction units. You need the software and the hardware, too. The hardware is a revenue source, and includes building rigs, building ships, building parks and barges, and building drilling rigs on the land and on the sea. To back all of this up, you need the software; you need banking; you need consultancy; and other software all of which helps draw revenue up the revenue scale.

Costs are the basket of land purchased or leased, taxes, fees, and so on, or any related levies under the legislation of the host government. All of this involves renting land from the host government, and perhaps putting together some infrastructure costs that involve consultancy, before you unlock the real investment revenue from the sale of the land.

Synergies is one of the most intellectually stimulating branches. Every hub needs the other hubs like members of an orchestra – delivering the 'sounds of success'. When you look at synergies, any kind of energy-related province or city will draw its strength and its weaknesses from the geography in which it is. It's like putting a strawberry seed in the earth – it will taste slightly different if you grow it in New Zealand than if you grow it in England. You need to be aware of the intricacies, the individual differences, and the possible enhancing of relationships between the hubs.

The Sunflower branch features large yellow petals. The petals represent the different countries, geographies and political systems involved in the Energy Province. Geographic locations have to dance with all their partners to the different tunes of anthropology.

What I am attempting to depict in this part of the Mind Map is the variation in focus and skill sets of the different nations and peoples, as well as the environments in which they traditionally work. For the flower of the project to blossom successfully, you must choose individuals and groups with skill sets that are specifically designed to help you with the vision of the project.

This is why the sunflower outlines, in the very colourful and bright way, the fact that differences are actually strengths. This branch of the Mind Map might be called the Harmony and Strength branch.

In summary, this is a Mind Map that describes how energy can be monetised. This involves energy in every sense – whether it is climate, human energy, money, anything – and shows how you can monetise these energies for the good of mankind.

Produced by Intelnacom – An Ideas Company: **www.intelnacom.com**

Mind Mapping is an excellent facilitator for strategic thinking; supporting and expanding on business tools and techniques from SWOT analysis to value chain analysis. Armed with a Mind Map of your company's objectives and a visual reminder of the direction in which you want the business to grow, success becomes much more attainable. Once you can see the bigger picture, you are able to concentrate on the smaller actions that will facilitate your attainment of that goal. Along the way you may need to make changes and promote your business to best effect, and the final part of this book will demonstrate how Mind Maps can help you do just this and achieve better business outcomes.

Mind Maps For Business Online

Many managers spend too much time thinking tactically and not enough time thinking strategically. It is vital that you see the 'whole picture'. The Mind Map allows you to do this. Complete some of the strategic thinking templates at **www.MindMapsForBusiness.com** to get an objective view of your organisation. You will also find articles, tips and how-to guides relating to this chapter.

nd Mapping for better business thinking

A Mind Map enables **everyone at every level** of the organisation to see the status quo, and **what is working** and what is not. I am **involving the staff** from the beginning of this process. By doing so, the problems are made **visible to everyone**. Everyone must be **engaged and committed** to co-create a viable structure that is **fair and transparent**.

Masanori Kanda, leading Japanese entrepreneur and Mind Mapper

Part 4
Mind Mapping for better business outcomes

Mind Mapping to increase sales

When I'm pitching I find people are often fascinated when I start mind mapping. It can become an 'ice-breaker' in its own right, as prospective or current clients chat away about the fact that they can't draw, or that more practical thinking skills should be taught in business. If you Mind Map in a meeting, the interesting thing is that you will have more time to look at the speaker – which in turn aids the listening process. And that's vital for better sales.

NIGEL TEMPLE, marketing consultant, trainer, speaker and author

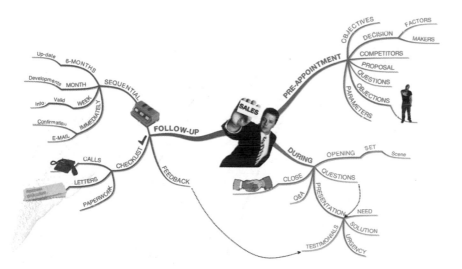

Mind Map summary for Chapter 11

Whether selling an idea, a product, or trying to gain the backing of your team or clients, how you pitch is crucial. Selling not only requires exceptional people skills, it also demands the mastery of a number of other competences, such as effective planning and time and information management. Whether you are selling to a private consumer or a large corporation, you are faced with increasingly large quantities of information that you must assemble, absorb, integrate and recall in an instant in order to convince people to buy from you. There are also several processes that you must coordinate in order to build long-lasting relationships with customers and prevent yourself losing potential sales.

Using Mind Maps can really help you become more strategic in your approach to sales and can clarify the way in which you handle your preparation, presentation and follow-ups. Using computer software for your Mind Mapping will make even more effective use of your time, skills and resources and will add a professional look to your Mind Maps.

Mind Mapping for sales

As with any business meeting, thorough preparation before your sales appointments is critical for achieving a good conversion rate of potential buyers into firm sales or orders. In order to prepare a first-rate sales presentation you must understand the needs and wants of your prospective buyers, understand their buying processes, collate information on your product or service, research competitors and combine all this knowledge to create an effective approach to your pitch.

A Mind Map acts as a supportive framework for your research, and once you have all the information you need in front of you, helps you prioritise issues and ideas to plan effectively. You can gather much of your research during the lead-generation and appointment-setting stages of the sales process, as well as by accessing general information sources such as industry reports, information on the prospect's website, forums, and so on. Generally, the larger the prospect, the more research you should do before your sales meeting. For instance, if your prospect represents a large organisation you will need to be more thoroughly prepared than if your prospect is a private consumer.

Using a Mind Map for your research also builds confidence as it ensures that you will come across as more knowledgeable when meeting with the prospect. You will have thought things through in a way that will help you respond optimally to your prospect's actions during the sales appointment.

Using a Mind Map to prepare for a sales appointment

First create a central theme (image and/or title) to symbolise the focus of your sales appointment. Add the main research points that you will investigate on central branches radiating out from this theme. To ensure your Mind Map preparation covers all angles, consider using the following topics for your main branches:

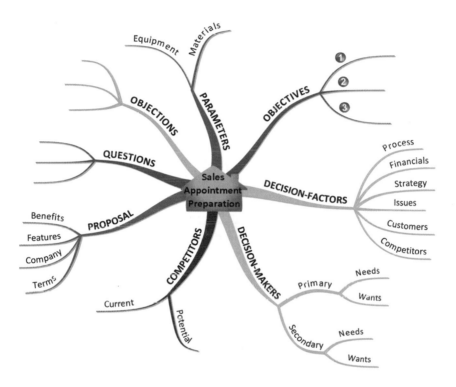

Objectives

Identify the main objectives and outcomes you would like to achieve from the sales appointment and prioritise them. These can vary dramatically depending on whether your appointment is with a private consumer or a large business. In the latter cases, the sale may involve multiple meetings with different people and objectives. For instance, at different stages you may aim to discover needs; raise awareness for the future; secure an order; set the stage for the next meeting; address any objections or concerns; set up another meeting with other key stakeholders; build relationships; and get commitment for the next steps.

The objectives that you set here will drive the content of your sales presentation.

Decision factors

Mind map the key factors that will affect the prospect's decision-making. Your sub-branches will include: Process – what sort of decision-making process is the prospect likely to follow? Financials – what are their financial parameters? For example: budgets, year-end date. Strategy – what are your prospect's strategic aims and priorities? Issues – are there any relevant issues, problems or challenges that may affect your prospect's decision-making? Customers – find out who your prospect's customers are. This is vital information to add to your understanding (and your Mind Map) about what their needs and issues might be. And finally, competitors. Who are your main competitors for your prospect's business?

If you can't discover this information prior to the appointment, try to determine what these factors generally are for the market sector in which the prospect operates. For private consumers, establish a Mind Map customer profile that will help you research the type of consumer that you have arranged to visit.

Decision makers

Determine as many of the prospect's personal or organisational decision makers and influencers as you can. This is important if you will be presenting to different people or groups, who will each have different personal and organisational needs and will therefore respond to different benefits. Highlight or clearly mark out who you feel is the primary decision maker. Try to assess thoroughly the needs and motives of your primary decision maker and secondary decision makers.

Understanding your prospect's needs in relation to the product or service that you are providing will help you develop a constructive sales approach so that their basic needs are completely satisfied. Needs determine the rational motives for buying the product. They are generally product-specific, relate to a situational problem and are based on facts that are often measurable. Evaluate how your product or service can meet basic needs, for example, by solving a specific problem, saving time or money or meeting an essential requirement.

Identifying your prospect's wants and needs in relation to your product or service is also crucial, as these determine the emotional and personal motives that drive buying behaviour and decisions. These are often based on perception, so consider how you can stimulate relevant buying motives to convince your prospect to buy from you. The most commonly referenced buying motives include desire for gain, fear of loss, comfort and convenience, security and protection, pride of ownership and satisfaction of emotion – all of these considerations should be mind mapped.

Competitors

Evaluate your current and potential competitors for the prospect's business. Discover what existing supply arrangements are in place for your type of product or service. Try to assess what the present supplier's reaction is likely to be if their business is under threat.

Consider too who else is likely to compete for the same prospect and what it is they are offering. Understanding this will help you decide how to make your company stand out from the competition.

Proposal

Using the insights gained from the research you have already undertaken, identify the main elements that will form your proposal.

Mind map the key benefits of the product or service that you feel will be most relevant to your prospect. Highlight or mark out the main or unique perceived benefit (personal or organisational) that your product or service would give to your prospect. This will be your main proposition, i.e. the major selling point for your presentation. For business decision makers, key benefits may relate to costs, profits and operating efficiency. Private consumers may also respond to the possibility that the decision will make them money, save money or time, as well as offer them more personal benefits such as improved image or greater security.

Summarise in a Mind Map the key features of your product or service to ensure that you are thoroughly up to speed with what you are offering. Briefly outline any key aspects of the product or service that you will need to actively demonstrate to the prospect.

Be prepared to give them the information that they need about you, too. In a Mind Map, jot down some key credibility points regarding yourself and the company you are representing that could be used to back up your proposal.

Define the pricing and contract terms for the sale in advance of your presentation and determine how far you would be willing to negotiate on them. Also, mind map any information you need to relate to the prospect regarding product implementation or installation.

Questions

Use this section of your Mind Map to prepare a checklist of questions or headings that will ensure you gather all the additional information you need at the appointment to fill in the gaps in your knowledge. Your questions should aim mainly to identify or confirm the strongest perceived personal or organisational benefit that the prospect would gain from your product or service.

You should also mind map any further questions that will help you discover how best to develop the sale with the individual or organisation; for example, how they decide, when, people and procedures involved, and competitor pressures. Ask them what their goals are, see if they are experiencing any problems, and if so, what are the consequences if the problem continues and how much is it costing them and their business? Find out if your prospect is in discussions with any other competitors and who in the organisation will be involved in choosing a supplier. Crucially, find out what your prospect's budget is and what room there is to negotiate on price.

Potential objections

No matter how effective you are at selling, you may still come across objections during your appointment. These must be handled constructively so as not to impede your progress. Think about the most likely ways your prospect will resist persuasion and the underlying reasons for their resistance. For example, their objection may result from doubt; a lack of resources, knowledge or finances; the absence of any real urgency or need, or simply because the prospect does not have the authority to make the final decision.

Go into your presentation prepared for these questions and on your Mind Map expand this section by connecting further sub-branches to plan your possible solutions and responses to each challenge.

Parameters

Under this main branch on your Mind Map, create further sub-topics to plan for additional factors that will ensure the smooth running of your presentation or meeting. For instance, the length of time that your presentation will take, any equipment requirements and the supporting materials that you will need to take with you: samples, hand-outs and brochures.

During the sales appointment

This stage is the execution of all your hard work in planning and preparing. Having arranged your sales visit for the purpose of presenting products or services or a specific proposal, you can ensure that a template Mind Map is prepared in advance to help you structure and record the entire visit. Using a Mind Map for the whole meeting is a great way to establish an open and engaging environment, perfect for eliciting your prospect's deepest requirements and encouraging their receptivity to your proposal.

The organic form of a Mind Map aids you in presenting a clear and concise picture of your proposal to your prospect in a way that is both compelling and memorable. It provides a great basis for a friendly exchange with your prospect. Indeed, the associative nature of a Mind Map will help you think creatively so that you can unlock your prospect's true needs and requirements and find ways to persuade them to your way of thinking.

Mind Mapping your sales meeting or presentation

On your completed Mind Map your main proposition will be clearly displayed as the central theme. Using a strong image for your central theme will really drive the proposition across to your prospect. The following main-branch topics provide a structured guideline for leading your prospect through the classic key sales steps.

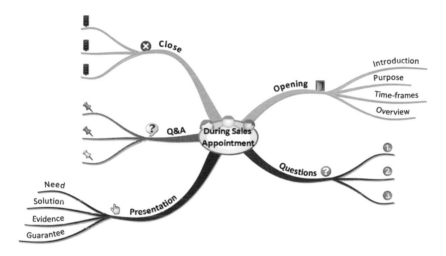

Opening

Introduce yourself. State your first and last name, the name of your company and the position in it that you hold, and briefly outline what your company does (ensure that this is tailored to appeal to your prospect). Set the scene by explaining the purpose of your visit; base this around your prospect, not yourself. For instance, indicate that you would like to learn about your prospect's situation and priorities in a particular area and to explain how your company approaches such issues. Then, if it looks as though there might be some common ground, agree how you could both move to the next stage.

Provide a quick outline of what you're going to talk about and how long it will take. Remember the importance of the 'recall during learning' principles (see page 99–100). Show your prospect your Mind Map, either on screen, as a print out, or both. It will act as a great ice-breaker and give you the opportunity to steer proceedings.

Ask your prospect how much time he or she has for the meeting and agree a time to finish that suits you both. Before you close the meeting, provide a quick credibility-building overview and review of yourself and your company and product or service.

Questions

Modern sales theory treats the questioning stage as an essential part of a facilitative process that helps the buyer make a decision, rather than just a process to assist the salesperson in gathering information. Your Mind Map can act as a supportive tool for opening up a channel of communication that will bring your prospect's true feelings, opinions, thoughts and needs into the open.

You will have prepared your questions or headings under this section of the Mind Map, so now use them to extract information from your prospect. Using good empathic questioning will help to build trust and rapport. You should listen carefully and show that you understand what the customer means and feels. While listening, try to identify all the strategic issues affected or implicated by the product or service in question, as these are where the ultimate decision-making and buying motives lie. Take the time to qualify and confirm what you have interpreted and summarise your prospect's key issues, requirements and priorities within this section of the Mind Map for later reference.

Presentation

This is the section of your Mind Map that will clearly and concisely demonstrate how your product or service or proposal meets the prospect's needs, priorities, constraints and motives.

The insights that you gained into the prospect's situation and priorities during the questioning phase are vital in order for you to highlight the most relevant points on your demonstration. Utilise your prepared Mind Map presentation along with any new information to match the benefits of the product with the needs of the prospect so that the prospect is entirely satisfied with the proposition.

The first main step in your presentation is to identify the fundamental problem or need that your prospect are experiencing. This is the whole basis on which your presentation will be leveraged as it provides the underlying motivation for them to buy your product. Consider what it is about their current situation that doesn't work and what issues surround their current solution, if there is one.

Having established the main problem or need, your goal now is to present your prospect with an ideal picture of how things will be when they never experience this problem again. Introduce them to the product, service or

Mind Mapping for better business outcomes

knowledge that you are offering and use emotional and logical points to show how it will resolve the problem. Trigger the motives that you identified during your research and through the questioning stage. Show how the features of the product and its associated advantages translate into actual benefits for the prospect. Pay particular attention to the main or unique perceived benefit of the product or service that you identified during your preparation. A good tip at this stage is to add urgency to your proposition by showing the prospect what will happen if they do not take action *now*, i.e. the implications of not purchasing the product or service.

Include evidence of success and other satisfied clients to back up the central proposition, such as customer testimonials and reference information, facts and figures. It is a good idea to prepare one key case study detailing the problem that a customer had, how your solution helped solve that problem and what the quantified benefits of your solution were.

Conclude the main body of your presentation by providing a powerful guarantee to give your prospect security and peace of mind. This is a good point at which to bring up your pricing information as you now have the strength of your presentation behind you. An attractive way to approach this is to show how long it will take a customer to recover the expenses of a purchase.

Q&A session (overcoming objections)

Successful modern selling now demands more initial understanding from the salesperson, so the need to overcome objections is not such a prevalent feature of the selling process. Nevertheless, objections do arise and they can be easily handled in a constructive and non-confrontational manner using Mind Maps.

Many objections are simply a request for more information and can be handled quickly. Respond to these as you would to any direct questions that your prospect may have. A powerful approach is to use relationship arrows to show how the benefits of your solution can meet the questions or objections that your prospect has raised.

With other, more complex objections it may be necessary to probe deeper to establish the precise nature of the objection, i.e. the real issue, and ensure there are no misunderstandings. A good technique for overcoming an objection is to isolate it by creating a branch for it on the Mind Map and then, along with the prospect, use free association to delve into what lies beneath each objection. You can then work together with the prospect to reshape the proposition so that it fits more acceptably with what is required. This productive method is a great way to avoid head-to-head confrontation and is excellent for relationship-building. Each objection can even be used as an opportunity to close the sale.

Once you've handled all questions and objections, your Mind Map will present an even stronger visual case for your prospect to proceed with the sale. The fact that you have both worked together to create the additional elements of the Mind Map also means that there is little possibility for misinterpretation in the next stage of the process.

Close

Once your prospect is happy that what you are selling will fulfil their needs, you will then be in a position to close the sale. How this works will depend on what you are selling and to whom you are selling it. For example, if you are selling a low-value item to a private individual, you'll want to finalise the deal or secure an order immediately. In these cases, conclude the deal by marking it out on the Mind Map along with the terms of agreement and how the arrangement will be implemented. Remember the 'recall during learning' principles.

However, if you are involved in a complex sale to a large organisation there may be other things that need to happen before you get a signed order form. If this is the case, make sure you understand and mind map what these steps are, who will be involved, and gain commitment on timeframes. Strong follow-up will be vital to convert this potential buyer into a firm customer.

The Mind Map format will work effectively no matter what the style of the decision maker. For instance, high-level, no-nonsense people are likely to decide very quickly and want all major matters mind mapped immediately with the detail to come later. Cautious, technical people may want to spend more time getting every small detail covered and this is easily catered for by adding more and more sub-branches to the Mind Map, or creating detailed 'child' Mind Maps.

Using Mind Map software during this stage really speeds up the conclusion of the meeting. There no longer needs to be a delay while confirmation of terms or arrangements are written up. Mind Maps can be quickly printed so both parties walk away with a fully signed-off record of the sale or a plan of action for what is to come.

Post-sales activity and follow-up

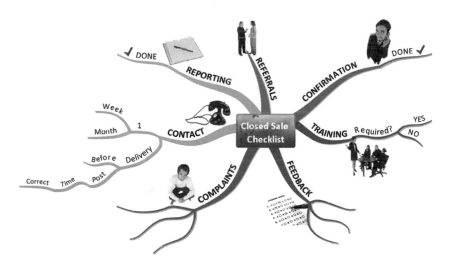

The level and nature of post-sales activity will depend on the type of product or service sold. It is generally understood that you must carry out a number of important processes to ensure customer value and satisfaction. Likewise, if you have not yet closed the sale, effective follow-up enables you to establish trust and is an important indicator of your integrity. Mind Maps can help you manage both of these aspects more strategically

Closed sale checklist

You can use a Mind Map to keep track of all the relevant after-sales processes you must undertake to manage the customer account effectively and fulfil your organisational requirements. In selling situations where repeat purchasing (not just a one off sale) is a goal, following up with the customer is critical to establishing a lucrative, long-lasting relationship.

Create main branches to ensure you have covered all the key points of the deal you have agreed and then, once back at the office, confirm all the details of the sale in an email or letter. Ensure that all relevant paperwork is completed and copies are provided to the customer, including any installation and delivery specifications and instructions.

Follow-up contact must be made with the customer as often as necessary to confirm that the customer is happy with the way the order is being processed. This helps reduce possible confusion that may result in customer dissatisfaction or order cancellation if left unresolved. Mind map regular calls at key stages to keep the customer informed before delivery and include a call after delivery. Check that they have received exactly what was agreed and on time.

Large, expensive business purchases may result in the salesperson spending considerable time with the client after the sale to help with any installation and training requirements. Smaller purchases may only require the salesperson to be available to answer queries once the customer starts to use the product.

Reporting and feedback is a necessary activity that is stipulated by the sales organisation and is often linked to sales commissions and bonuses. Use your Mind Map as a project management tool to track your reporting information, such as the order value, product type and quantity, and other relevant details about the customer.

Record any problems or complaints raised by the customer and mind map your progress in solving them. Note down any feedback – positive and negative – you receive from the customer. You can utilise positive feedback as a testimonial to help you gain more sales. Any negative feedback presents an opportunity for you and the company you represent to make improvements.

Good conscientious follow-up will usually be rewarded with referrals to other customers. Ask for recommendations from your customer to open up new sales opportunities.

The 'contact' branch: following up potential sales with Mind Maps

It is absolutely critical to keep yourself in the potential buyer's mind after your sales appointment, otherwise you may lose out on completing the transaction. One of the best ways that Mind Maps help you do this is by establishing strong recall. As already noted, research shows that you lose 80 per cent of the detail you have learned within 24 hours of having learned it (see also pages 99–100). However, if you review information using a Mind Map within 24 hours of learning it, you should be able to retain virtually everything. If you then review regularly using a Mind Map you can keep retention consistently high.

In the light of this, it is a good idea to set up a sequenced follow-up campaign based on a Mind Map summary of key information from your sales visit. It is recommended that you contact the potential buyer at the following intervals until you get a result:

- **Immediately after the meeting** – Write a letter confirming your meeting and the outcome as soon as you are able to do so and attach a Mind Map summary for the potential buyer's reference. Send it via email or fax so that there is a greater possibility of the prospect reviewing it within 24 hours.

- **Within one week** – Contact the prospect via the telephone with a valid reason that provides a step forward in the sales process, not just to ask if they've made a purchasing decision. For instance, you may have the results of the research that you agreed to do at the sales appointment or you may need to get clarification on something.

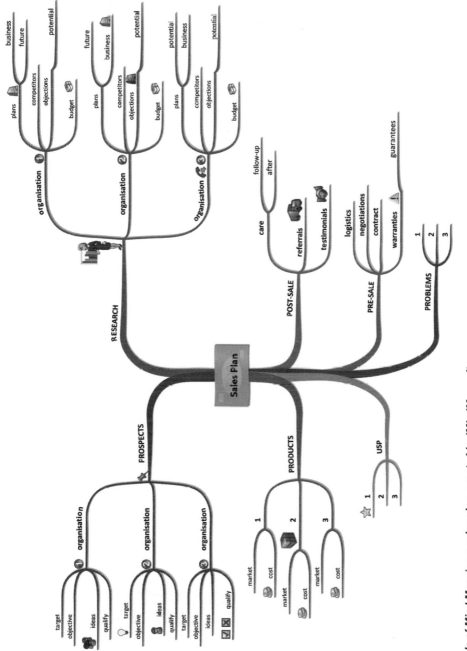

An example of Mind Mapping a sales plan, created by iMindMap software

You should then resend your Mind Map summary via email or fax to remind them of the key benefits of your proposition. You can even add the updated information to the Mind Map to illustrate how your relationship is progressing.

- **Within one month** – If you have still not succeeded in closing the sale, contact the prospect again a month later with any new information or developments that may influence their purchase decision. Otherwise, provide them with news of a special sale or new catalogue, etc. Use this contact as another opportunity to move things forward. Again, supply a Mind Map reminder of your proposition to keep yourself at the forefront of their mind.

- **Within six months** – Even though it may seem that the sale is definitely not going to proceed at this stage, it is still a good idea to keep the prospect up to date with any new information that could eventually tip them over into purchasing. They will already be very familiar with your Mind Map and your proposition; therefore if their situation changes and they are in a better position to buy, it is highly likely that you will be their first port of call.

Well thought out and structured follow-ups demonstrate your determination to develop a relationship with your potential client, and most significant sales are usually the end result of a relationship that has been developed over time. Even if many of your prospects are not interested, quite a few potential buyers will appreciate the extra effort and you will be rewarded in the end. In the long run, sales follow-ups are much more cost-effective than sourcing new customers from scratch.

Mind Maps are an important element of any sales presentation; creating a Mind Map before a presentation allows you to prepare your ideas and formulate a strategy which will help you to appear confident in your ideas or product. It is this sort of authority and conviction that will win over your clients on the day. Of course, as in any situation where negotiating a deal is concerned (see Chapter 5), you need to stay focused on your end goal and be flexible enough to compromise, should the situation demand it. The final chapter of this book invites you to look at your own goals and to see how you can best achieve them to maximise your business potential.

Mind Maps For Business Online Optimise the way you handle sales preparation, presentations and follow-ups to improve your closure rate. Try the templates that can be found at **www.MindMapsForBusiness.com** the next time you have a big sales pitch to deliver. You will find articles, tutorials, tips and how-to guides relating to optimising your sales.

Mind Mapping to set goals and embrace change

Mind Maps have made it easier to manage goals, create action plans and enhance our planning abilities.

THE SPORTS MANAGERS COLLEGE, operated by the Japan Football Association

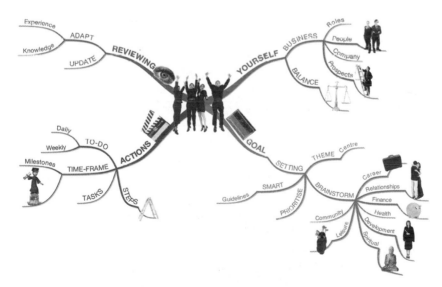

Mind Map summary for Chapter 12

All 'intelligence workers' need to strike a balance between their professional and their personal lives that will allow you to pursue your dreams, achieve your goals, and enjoy time with family and friends. Setting clear priorities and goals for the future is a fundamental step towards achieving a well-balanced life. Constructive goal-setting using Mind Maps can help you regain control of your life.

More and more people are struggling to maintain a balance between the personal, business and social aspects of their lives. With recent developments in technology, globalisation, changing family roles and increasing productivity expectations, the boundaries between work and personal life are becoming blurred. The imbalance that results can cause tension and anxiety for many people, compromising their enjoyment of life. It is easy to conclude that you can never do enough in any area of your life when you feel torn between your job, personal pursuits and family.

To bring about more effective change in your business or work, bear in mind that you are much more in control than you may have thought. Whatever the change you are considering or experiencing, you always have the option of adopting a proactive persona, focusing on the percentage that is good in the situation, while still being quite realistic about the fact that a further percentage of your situation is pretty awful and needs changing.

So what are the different aspects of business that are acting upon you from your outer to inner circles of influence? They include global business and forward trends, national changes in the political and economic arenas, political influences at home and abroad, environmental fluctuations, both natural and man-made, corporate business and levels of profit, and financial factors in investments and commercial trends. More direct influences at work include the leadership of the organisation, divisional management, team behaviour, your relationships with colleagues and also your own personal vision of yourself.

A Mind Map of the aspects of business that act upon you

Mind Mapping for better business outcomes

No matter how senior or junior you are in your company, you have influence at every level of the organisation within which you work, and you can make a difference whatever the stage you are at in your career.

Mind Mapping yourself in business

Whatever the change you are planning or facing, you will want to take stock of where you are and where you are heading in your career or work. Focusing first on your current job or your desired position, select an image that is representative of your feelings about the goal in the centre of your page. Decide on the branches for the Mind Map, based on considerations of following questions:

- What are the major elements in your professional life?

- What is your actual job?

- What are your goals within it?

- What are your satisfactions within it?

- What are your dissatisfactions within it?

- Who are your friends and colleagues?

- Who are your 'change master' groups?

- What is your environment like?

- Is your income satisfactory and is it growing fast enough?

- Are your colleagues people whom you enjoy working with?

- Is the vision of your company consistent with your personal visions?

- Are your bosses people whom you respect, look up to and who help you and nurture you?

- What are your strengths and weaknesses, and what are the opportunities within your career path?

- What are the threats to your chosen career path?

- Are you seeking promotion – or no promotion?

- Is the company liable to be taken over? Will there be redundancies?

- If you are seeking a new job, what do you want from that new job?

Make sure that the 'you' you are developing remains strong, healthy and focused by planning for time with friends, family or leisure pursuits outside your work commitments. It is very important to integrate your life goals with your professional goals, rather than allowing them to develop in conflict with each other.

Mind Mapping to achieve balance – goal setting

Using Mind Maps to set out your goals brings you the clarity you need to find direction and choose where you want to go in life. By tapping into your inner feelings, you can use Mind Maps to dispel any internal conflicts and set sharp, clearly defined priorities for all areas of your life. By knowing precisely what you want to achieve in your life, you can concentrate your time, effort and resources accordingly, and access your natural reserves of motivation.

With your goals clearly mind mapped in an instantly visible, clear fashion, you will be able to spot and quickly dismiss any distractions that could steer you away from your desired course. What's more, as you start achieving your goals, you'll find that your self-confidence in your ability to manage your life will build quickly.

How to set goals using Mind Maps

The flexibility of Mind Maps allows you to set goals on a number of different levels. If you prefer to draw by hand, first sketch a Mind Map of your desires and wishes as well as your responsibilities and constraints. You can then review this and work up a more polished, considered and colourful Mind Map. Alternatively, you can use Mind Map software which will give you a natural visual representation of your goals, and you can easily adjust or re-group your goals with just a few clicks of the mouse. You can also drill down further into your Mind Map for more detailed planning.

When you put your hopes and dreams down on paper, first create your 'big picture' of what you want to do in the long term; that is, the large-scale goals you want to achieve. Next, you can break these down into the small-scale targets or actions that you must meet to reach your large-scale goals. You can even outline your goals in a series of Mind Maps which, when combined, will make a 'life dashboard Mind Map' for managing all areas of your life.

The following process provides you with guidelines for creating a Mind Map to set out your goals and the actions required to achieve them.

1 Create your central 'goals' theme

The first step is to create a central theme to represent your goals. An effective tip is to base your central theme on the extent of your goal-setting. For instance, are you looking to create lifetime goals, ten-year goals, five-year goals, or simply goals for the coming year or month?

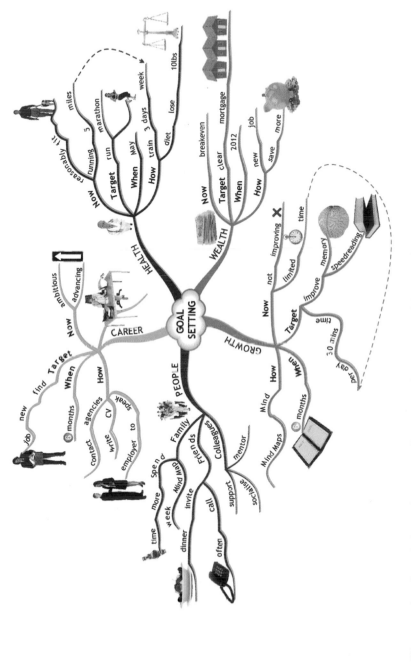

Use life categories when mind mapping your goals to ensure that you are looking at the 'big picture'

Setting goals for a long-term period gives you an overall perspective that can better shape all other aspects of your decision-making. Your long-term vision will inspire you to attain greater efficiency and application in your daily life.

2 Brainstorm your main goals

Next, spend as much time as you need to brainstorm your main goals, i.e. the large-scale goals for each area of your life. Place them on central branches radiating out from your central theme. The mind-mapping format encourages you to create and visualise your goals in the context of all the major areas in your life, thus helping you achieve improved balance. Use images where possible to represent your goals, as this makes them more compelling. Consider the following major life roles or domains for categorising your goals:

- **Career and business** – Think about what level you want to reach in your current career, or perhaps changing careers? If you are running your own business, what are your desired levels of market share, profit, service and quality in the long term?

- **Family and relationships** – How do you want your relationship with your partner to develop? Do have any goals in relation to being a parent or improving your parenting skills? What sort of relationship do you want with your extended family and friends?

- **Wealth and finances** – What are your goals regarding your personal finances? How much do you want to earn by a particular stage? Do you have any goals for gaining passive income?

- **Physical and health** – Are there any athletic or health goals that you want to achieve? For instance, do you want to lose a certain amount of weight or establish a specific physical training programme?

- **Growth and personal development** – Is there any particular knowledge, education or training that you want to acquire? What information and skills will you need to achieve other goals? For instance, you may want to learn a language or develop your abilities at public speaking.

- **Spiritual** – What level do you want to be spiritually? What goals do you have for improving your spirituality? For example, do you want to learn to meditate or become involved in a particular spiritual or religious community?

- **Leisure** – How do you want to enjoy yourself? Are there any hobbies you want to develop? What sort of travel goals do you have?

- **Contribution and community** – How do you want to make the world a better place? Are there any community services that you would like to participate in?

If you are setting your goals from a long-term perspective, you may find it necessary to break down your longer goals into sub-goals as an aid to better planning. For example, if you are setting five-year goals, you can break these down into smaller yearly goals that you will need to achieve in order to reach your five-year goals.

3 Prioritise and connect your goals

Once you have created all your goals, assign every goal within each category a priority ranking, either critical or important, desirable, or just nice to have.

Additionally, or alternatively, select the key goals from across the Mind Map that best reflect what you want to achieve overall and add symbols, numbers or icons (such as clouds) over them to highlight their importance.

Consider trimming your goals until you have a smaller number of especially significant ones on which you can really focus; try not to exceed five goals per area. (This is easier to do using Mind Map software as you can just delete any extraneous goals from your Mind Map.) Make sure that the goals you end up with are ones that you genuinely wish to achieve, not ones that other people in your life might want you to achieve.

Prioritising your goals in this way prevents you from feeling overwhelmed by too many goals and directs your attention to the most important ones. You will also probably see some common threads across all your goals – link these with lines and arrows to establish a connection between them.

How to survive the global financial crisis with a Mind Map: C. C. Thum's story

Like many people worried about the economic environment, C.C. Thum from Singapore realised he needed to expedite an action plan to meet the looming crisis. Creating a Mind Map helped him cope with a big change, the loss of his job.

The global financial turmoil has finally impacted me in a direct way. I was not only told I was being made redundant but that my last day of service was that same day. I couldn't believe that this had happened to me.

I had used Mind Maps before and decided I needed to mind map what was happening to me and how I could cope with the changes. One Mind Map which I had drawn back in 2006 unwittingly came back to guide me. It was a Mind Map of life goals that I had created after attending a Buzan Mind Map seminar. At the time I could visualise my 'retirement' and the action required to achieve the desired outcome. I also realised that I enjoyed Mind Mapping thoroughly. However, my job was always given priority and my time spent on Mind Maps was rather restricted. Nonetheless, I continued to pursue my dreams and passion.

With redundancy and the dearth of jobs in the financial industries, my priority has now shifted to Mind Mapping and training others how to use it. The secret to surviving redundancy is in the Mind Map. Key ideas are visualised and drawn into the Mind Map. On reflection I realised that Mind Maps actually saved me from constantly worrying about my future and questioning the reasons for being made redundant.

C.C. Thum's Mind Map of reviewing goals after redundancy

4 Make goals SMART

At this stage it is a good idea to introduce SMART (specific, measurable, achievable, realistic, time-based) guidelines to ensure your goals are as powerful as possible. It is important to be precise and include dates, times, targets and amounts so that you will be able to measure your achievement. You should also take care to set outcomes that you can realistically achieve and over which you have as much control as possible. With this in mind, add detail on the 'who, what, when, where and why' elements that are necessary to achieve each goal on your Mind Map.

- **Who** – Who is involved? For example, you, your partner, a member of your family, your boss, etc.

- **What** – What exactly do you want to accomplish? Try to be specific regarding any targets or amounts.

- **When** – Establish a timeframe.

- **Where** – Identify a location such as your home, workplace, gym, and so on.

- **Why** – Outline your specific reason(s) for wanting to pursue the goal or the benefits you will gain by accomplishing the goal.

Actions

Now you are ready to outline the steps and actions that you will take to achieve your goals within each life category of your Mind Map. If your goal-setting Mind Map becomes cluttered at this stage, consider creating new, secondary Mind Maps where you can focus on detailed action planning for each category.

Branching out directly from your goals, break down the tasks that you need to carry out to achieve each goal. If you want to go into further detail, you can set timeframes or milestones for your tasks that measure your progress. For instance, if you are goal-setting for one year, you can organise your tasks according to a six-month plan, one-month plan and even a weekly plan of progressively smaller targets that you should attain to reach your overall goal for the year.

You can also attach numerical rankings to the actions in your plans, making it easy to see the order in which you need to complete each task.

By allowing you to explore your goals in depth, your Mind Map can help you handle your time efficiently to focus on the basic steps that will lead you to achieve your larger goals.

Seeing all the tasks you assign for a specific goal in Mind Map format can help you improve the quality of your goal-setting. It is easy to work out whether any of the dates you have set are achievable or if you are overcommitting yourself in any particular area.

You can use Mind Map software both to define your action plans and also to monitor and track your progress. Many mind-mapping programs enable you to attach dates or deadlines to branches and you can even see the percentage of completion you have achieved for each action item in your plans.

'To-do' Mind Maps

You can go even further and create a daily or weekly 'to-do' Mind Map of the things that you should do to work towards your main goals (for examples of 'to-do' Mind Maps, see Chapter 4). This will help to improve the practicality of your goal-setting as you will quickly identify any changing priorities or experiences. You can then adjust your main 'goals' Mind Map to reflect these changes. What's more, as Mind Mapping paves the way for a free flow of ideas and associations, you could end up discovering new and innovative ways to reach your goals.

Reviewing your goals

Your goals will change as time progresses. It is important to review your 'goal' Mind Map and modify it to take into account any growth in your knowledge or experience. On a more ongoing basis, maintain the balance in your life by updating your action plans or 'to-do' Mind Map regularly.

Every time you achieve a goal, review and adjust your Mind Map from your new perspective. For instance, if you achieved the goal too easily, make your next goal in that area more challenging. However, if the goal took a disheartening amount of time and effort to achieve, make the next goal a little easier. If you fail to meet your goals, don't be discouraged, just learn from your experience and feed any lessons gained back into your Mind Map. If particular goals no longer hold any attraction, then simply remove them from your Mind Map and focus your attention on goals that you are still eager to achieve.

Fine-tuning the goal-setting process with Mind Maps

Here is a Mind Map story outlining the results of Mind Map implementation at the Japan Football Association Sports Managers College.

The Sports Managers College (SMC) operated by the Japan Football Association (JFA) provides an environment to study management of sporting organisations and is involved in educating personnel responsible for the future development of the sporting world and the further establishment of sporting culture. SMC offers a full course and satellite course (a 24-hour course consisting of eight sessions of three hours per session). The Mind Map technique has been incorporated into both of these programmes.

Nurturing individuality is one of the most important objectives for those of us operating the SMC programmes. Naturally, the game of soccer is also important, and since no one ever knows what will happen in the crucial 45 minutes of each half of a soccer match, each player has to continually judge conditions, figure out what they need to do and move accordingly. In other words, the players are not managed by anyone, and have to read and manage the situation on the pitch by themselves. I think that the situation on the ground in organisational management is the same. The important thing is the individual's ability to select the best tactics to respond to the situation at hand, and since the Mind Map technique dovetails with this SMC concept, we have included it in our programmes. The main results of its implementation are summarised below.

Subjectively formulating visions

The importance of vision in management is often talked about, and at SMC we also recognise that the process of accurately assessing current situations, deciding upon future targets and then acting to achieve those targets, or goals, is the central role of management. However, we feel that simply using borrowed words or flowery phrases to create run-of-the-mill mission statements or visions does not really empower people to realise actual goals. Moreover, against the backdrop of the Japanese postwar education system, many Japanese people feel uneasy about subjective goal-setting in such an unresponsive society. For this reason we have considered ways of bringing out individuality within the goal-setting process.

It is clear to us that individuality in goal-setting has improved greatly since we began using the Mind Map. We believe this is because individuals are constantly, freely and subjectively making abundant 'selections' of words, icons, colours, thickness and sizes, depth and placement of items on the page during the actual Mind Map drawing process. Through the practice of this free and subjective selection process, this useful tool gets individuals to look intently at themselves, their beliefs and dreams, and further use their imagination to look at the various interconnected aspects of the current conditions and history of their local society, and so forth. We discovered that getting individuals to formulate goals subjectively in this way enhances the motivation required to take action towards realising those goals.

Thinking about solutions

One of the main SMC objectives is to make people happy through a life enriched by sport. In considering this aim, we understand that it is not enough for an individual to have a self-centred vision of how that individual would like to be in the future. Individuals must also consider ways to make others in the world 'outside' themselves happy. In other words, this is a solution. So, first of all, the individual needs to find out what the issues are outside and then consider measures to resolve them.

Simply put, people need to consider the situations of others. We have found that in order to achieve this it is important to create hypothetical plans freely in one's own mind and then try to obtain some verification (although it is impossible to be the other person). If an individual loses autonomy, active discovery of issues in the individual's environment ceases, and consequently forward-looking solutions for those external problems may fail to appear. In one way, the service of other people's mentality could be viewed as a form of meddling in others' affairs, but we prefer to think of it as a source of innovative solutions. We hold the view that the continued use of free creativity involved in drawing the Mind Map has the potential to train people in this positive approach to the surrounding environment that is needed to bring forth such solutions. We think of the Mind Map as a lubricant that frees the imagination to process external information, and smoothly formulate and verify ideas in one's own mind.

Planning

Planning takes place once current situations are understood and future goals established, and action plans can be devised from a clear global perspective of the desired outcomes. In particular, various things are really interlinked in the recognition of current situations and future goals.

At such times creativity is required to grasp such a holistic image efficiently and, through the use of the Mind Map, planners are able to create an instant overall image, allocate priorities, and then put these together into a single story that we can call a business plan. We believe the introduction of Mind Maps has made it easier to manage goals and devise action plans and has also enhanced planning ability.

Creating a collaborative environment

In what could be called a team-building function and perhaps a secondary effect of the Mind Map implementation, we found that getting attendees to focus on their uniqueness and express their individuality seemed to dissolve the usual boundaries of age, sex or rank. This resulted in the creation of a freer, more comfortable atmosphere of equality in the study environment at SMC.

Freely expressing individuality through the Mind Map enables people to recognise the fact that they are naturally different. In addition, it enables us at SMC more easily to recognise the common objectives required for advancement through sports management study. This also fosters the self-reliance and mutual aid that are necessary for the formation of club culture, which is an aim at SMC. Course participants who may feel the stressful undercurrents of the rigid tendencies of Japanese educational institutions, workplaces and society in general, will certainly feel comfortably released in this atmosphere of equality and freedom.

Becoming a supportive and creative person

Just like the game of soccer, the management of sporting organisations and all kinds of tasks relating to such organisations can be called creative arts for the people working in those areas. With its overflowing colours, interplay between icons and illustrations and expressive curved lines, the Mind Map enables people to articulate freely their inner world as an art form with abundant individuality. For us, this begins with people who have come together with a common love of the free sport of soccer, and encourages people to complete tasks in a freer and more artistic way.

The 2005 JFA mission statement advocates the following vision for the future: 'To help create a society in which sport plays a role in enhancing people's happiness by broadening the appeal of soccer and making sport more accessible.' At JFA, we believe the driving force behind realising this goal is the grassroots energy coming from people in all regions who love soccer and are involved with the many aspects of the game (at JFA we call this the 'soccer family'). Our hope is to use this energy to vitalise the soccer world, the sports world and our country, by shining a light on previously repressed individuality and encouraging each member of the soccer family to perform their job with artistic originality. The Mind Map is an effective tool for revealing uniqueness and individuality in those people.

SMC course subjects where Mind Maps are used include:

- Mind Map fundamentals
- environmental analysis
- product development
- business concepts
- vision
- SWOT
- action planning
- goal management.

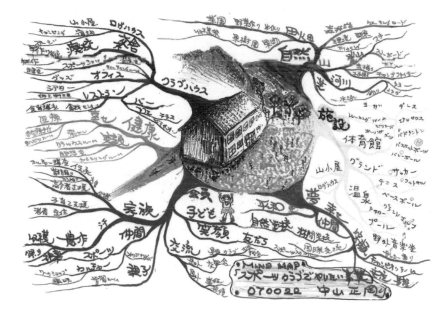

Photos of Mind Maps and ideas used by the Japan Football Association

Through these and other Mind Map stories we have sprinkled throughout the book, and with the diverse business applications we have shown step by step, we hope we have demonstrated that Mind Maps really are better for business. We leave you with this story. Enjoy your work, enjoy your life, enjoy Mind Maps to get the best from both worlds.

Work–life balance

My Mind Map describes my ideal work–life balance. The Mind Map is filed in my day planner with other important Mind Maps (about vision, mission, and so on) so that I can refer to it frequently. This helps me not to lose sight of my life goals even during the very hectic hours and days. I started mind mapping for survival (or efficiency) almost 25 years ago. As a long-time Mind Mapper, I strongly believe that the benefit of using Mind Maps far exceeds my initial success at school.

MIKIKO CHIKADA KAWASE

Mikiko Chikada Kawase's Mind Map of achieving a work–life balance

Using Mind Mapping to set your goals is an immensely powerful and meaningful way to decide what is important for you to achieve in your life. Instead of aimlessly trying to fit everything in, Mind Mapping your goals encourages you to see the 'big picture' and coordinate all categories of your life from a high-level perspective. From this basis, you can then organise your time and resources to achieve all your significant goals and avoid unnecessary distractions in your life. As you make Mind Mapping your goals a part of your life, you will strike the right balance between all the demands on your time and benefit from positive advancements in all areas of your life.

Mind Maps For Business Online   President Barak Obama said 'We are the ones we've been waiting for. We are the change that we seek'. Embracing change is good, so click on the link to www.MindMapsForBusiness.com to find articles, iMindMap tutorials, tips and how-to guides on achieving that work-life equilibrium.

Conclusion

The success of many businesses over the last decade can mainly be attributed to the information worker – MBAs, computer programmers, accountants, lawyers, IT workers, etc. – but things are about to change. The age of the whole-brain thinker, those individuals that use both left and right hemispheres of the brain, has now dawned. These will become the most influential, and thus most valuable, people in any organisation. It will be the individuals that can think creatively to solve problems, find solutions, add value, and enable innovation who will be the trendsetters for the next decade. Information is now cheap. We can find out what we need to know, when we need to know it. We no longer need information managers, we need to learn how to better manage the managers of knowledge – the human brain!

Aristotle believed that the metaphor was the highest form of thinking and thought it 'a sign of genius'. How can we use this to our benefit? Well, if a picture is worth a thousand words, and a metaphor is worth a thousand pictures, the Mind Map is the metaphoric representation of our thoughts in a visual form that fully duplicates the non-linear, organic nature of human thought.

Businesses are built around systems, but how many companies have systems in place to enable employees to think in the most effective way? Ask any chief executive why his or her company has achieved success and they will tell you it is because of their 'people'. If people are the most important element of any business, what is the most important element of every person? Quite clearly we are what we think, and if we think better, we can be more efficient, creative and productive. Therefore, if you are part of an organisation that does not have a thinking system in place, get your colleagues mind mapping. Not to do so would be doing them a great disservice.

Throughout the chapters in this book we've shown you another, better way to perform in business through the use of Mind Maps, and demonstrated how you can use them to best exploit your own potential and that of your colleagues. We hope that you can now recognise the importance of Mind Maps for decision-making, organising your own ideas and those of others, thinking creatively as well as for advanced brainstorming, improving your memory and imagination. You have now been given the tools with which you can confidently address all these business situations and demands in a thorough and highly efficient manner. Once you've mastered the mind-mapping technique yourself and have witnessed the benefits of the system, you will understand how it can revolutionise your business when used by the whole team.

As technology has progressively taken an ever more dominant role in business, Mind Mapping has had to follow this trend, and for those who work predominantly on screen, the iMindMap program has proved invaluable. Whether Mind Maps are originated on screen or on paper and then transferred to the computer, the ability to project Mind Maps, email them or place them on central servers enables information to be shared with colleagues and clients with ease and clarity. The case studies we have given you will illustrate how Mind Maps can be used within your business, and demonstrate just how effective they can be.

The iMindMap software and Mind Maps are used by tens of thousands of individuals in organisations all over the world to help them plan, create, problem solve, present and much more. Here are just a few: A Hermes, Accenture, BBC, BP, British Army, British Telecom, BSkyB, Centrica, Daimler, De Beers, Deep Sea Asia, Friends of the Earth, Harper Collins, Hess Ltd, Hong Kong Institute for Design, HP, HSBC, IBM, Intel, International Rugby Board, ITG, ITV Plc, Johnson Controls, Ladbrokes, Merrill Lynch, Microsoft, NASA, NHS, Nissan, Oxford University Press, Pearson, Phillips Innovation, Pizza Hut, Procter and Gamble, Reuters, RNIB, Saga, Rolls-Royce plc, Save the Children, Scholastic, Singapore Institute of Management, Smith & Nephew, Target, Tec, Tesco, Toyota, Unichem, US Air Force, Vodafone, Walt Disney, The Wrigley Company Ltd, Yum.

Armed with all the information you need to use your whole brain you can really exploit your creativity using Mind Maps and make your business a success, now and in the future. Technology has an important place in the modern business, but as we leave the Information Age and enter the Age of Intelligence, nothing is as effective as the human brain. Use it well, and reap the rewards.

Appendix

 At **www.imindmap.com** you will discover the official mind-mapping software website in which Tony Buzan's world famous and original Mind Maps®, now in version 4.0, is replicated and expanded. This is the closest a desktop or laptop computer, or even an iPhone or other pda, can come to reflecting the imagination and association processes of true Mind Mapping carried out so effortlessly by that other ultimate computer, the human brain. **www.imindmap.com** includes:

Videos

Articles

Tutorials

Mind-mapping tips

iMindMap templates

How-to guides

Tony Buzan's 'Festival of the Mind' online resources

The Festival of the Mind is a showcase event for the five learning 'mind sports' of Memory, Speed Reading, IQ, Creativity and Mind Mapping.

The first Festival was held in the Royal Albert Hall in 1995 and was organised by Tony Buzan and Raymond Keene OBE. Since then, the Festival has been held in the UK, alongside the World Memory Championships in Oxford, and in other countries around the world including Malaysia, China and Bahrain. The interest from the public in all the five learning mind sports is growing worldwide so, not surprisingly, the Festival is a big attraction. In fact, an event devoted solely to Mind Maps with Tony Buzan filled the Albert Hall again in 2006.

Each of the mind sports has its own Council to promote, administer and recognise achievement in its field.

The World Memory Sports Council

The World Memory Sports Council is the independent governing body of the Mind Sport of Memory and regulates competitions worldwide. Tony Buzan is the President of Council. You can visit the site at **www.worldmemorysports council.com**.

The World Memory Championships

This is the pre-eminent national and international memory competition where records are continually smashed. For instance, in the 2007 UK Memory Championships Ben Pridmore memorised a single shuffled deck of playing cards in 26.28 seconds beating the previous World Record of 31.16 seconds set by Andi Bell (for years, memorising a pack of cards in under 30 seconds has been seen as the memory equivalent of beating the four minute mile in athletics). Full details of the World Memory Championships can be found on the website **www.worldmemorychampionships.com** with its interactive Mind Map designed by Mind Map World Champion Phil Chambers using Buzan's iMindMap.

Memory Championships for Schools

Since it was founded in 1991, the World Memory Championships has created a 'gold standard' for memory based on ten different memory disciplines. A simplified version of these has now been created specifically for schools memory competitions, backed up with a training programme to help teachers to train memory techniques. In a nationwide educational partnership, consisting of the UK Memory Sports Council, Inspire Education, and national government initiative Aimhigher, students are taught powerful memory techniques which, when put into practice, can provide the intellectual platform for recalling almost anything, instantly. They are passing on these techniques to teachers and pupils at secondary schools throughout the UK – by means of the UK Schools Memory Championships.

Organised by Inspire Education and spearheaded by eight times World Memory Champion Dominic O'Brien and the Chief Arbiter of the World Memory Championships, Phil Chambers, the UK Schools Memory Competition has been created to help pupils discover the mind sport of memory and to develop their mental skills to help their studies. We are in the process of creating a model here in the UK which can be repeated around the world with the goal of eventually establishing the 'World Schools Memory Championships' soon after 2010. For more information, log onto **www.schoolsmemorychampionships.com**.

buzan Welcome to TONY BUZAN's world. Tony Buzan is the inventor of Mind Maps – the most powerful 'thinking tool' of our times. Discover more about Tony himself, and the transformative powers of MIND MAPPING, MEMORY and SPEED READING at **www.buzanworld.com**.

 The World Speed Reading Council was established to promote, train and recognise achievements in the field of Speed Reading worldwide. Apart from developing the ability to gain an understanding of large quantities of text in a short time, Speed Reading is one of the five learning 'mind sports' which can be practised competitively. Their website is **www.worldspeedreadingcouncil.com**.

 Mind Mapping is a 'Thought Organisation Technique' invented by the international author and expert on the brain, Tony Buzan, in 1971. The World Mind Mapping Council administers and promotes the sport and also awards the prestigious title of Mind Mapping World Champion. The current reigning World Champion is Phil Chambers. Visit the site at **www.worldmindmappingcouncil.com**.

 The Worldwide Brain Club, set up by the Buzan Organisation, encourages the formation of Brain Clubs worldwide. These have flourished for many years and bring together Mind Mapping, Creativity, IQ, Speed Reading and Memory. Practising each of these disciplines positively impacts on the others. Using Mind Maps, for example, helps with creativity as it presents ideas in a brain-friendly way that inspires new ideas. Working on memory techniques makes the brain more capable in every other area in the same way as working out in a gym builds muscles.

Brain Clubs, whether set up in a school or college, or within an organisation or company, create a supportive environment where all the members share the same objective: to give their personal 'neck top computer' the best operating system possible. Buzan Centres worldwide provide qualified trainers in all of these areas. See **www.buzanworld.com** and **www.world brainclub.com**.

The Brain Trust is a registered charity which was founded in 1990 by Tony Buzan with one objective: to maximise the ability of each and every individual to unlock and deploy the vast capacity of his or her brain. Its charter includes promoting research into study of thought processes, the investigation of the mechanics of thinking, manifested in learning, understanding, communication, problem-solving, creativity and decision-making. In 2008 Professor (Baroness) Susan Greenfield won its 'Brain of the Century' award. Visit **www.braintrust.org.uk**.

The International Academy of Mental World Records at **www.mentalworldrecords.com** exists to recognise the achievements of Mental Athletes around the world. In addition to arbiting world record attempts and awarding certificates of achievement, the Academy is also linked to the International Festival of the Mind, which showcases mental achievements in the five learning mind sports of Memory, Speed Reading, Creativity, Mind Mapping and IQ.

Creativity is defined by Torrance, the doyen of creativity testing, as follows:

'Creativity is a process of becoming sensitive to problems, deficiencies, gaps in knowledge, missing elements, disharmonies and so on; identifying the difficulty; searching for solutions; making guesses or formulating hypotheses about the deficiencies; testing and re-testing these hypotheses and possibly modifying and retesting them; and finally communicating the results.'

Creativity is one of the five learning mind sports along with Mind Mapping, Speed Reading, IQ and Memory.

All of these skills positively impact on the others and together they can help any individual to be more effective in whatever they choose to do. All five learning mind sports are featured in the Festival of the Mind. Visit **www.worldcreativitycouncil.com**.

Intelligence Quotient (IQ) is one of the five learning 'mind sports' which include Mind Mapping, Creativity, Speed Reading and Memory.

The World IQ Council can be contacted at **www.worldiqcouncil.com** and you can test your IQ on this site as well.

Index

Unleash the power of your mind with these bestselling titles from the world's leading authority on the brain and learning...

The original and the best book on Mind Maps from their world-renowned inventor.

ISBN 9781406647167

Embark on the most exciting intellectual adventure of your life and discover how easy it is to supercharge your memory.

ISBN 9781406644265

Revolutionise the way you read with the ultimate guide to reading, understanding and learning at amazing speeds.

ISBN 9781406644296